Mometrix
TEST PREPARATION

ASCS®

I0889401

Exam Secrets

Study Guide

Dear Future Exam Success Story

First of all, **THANK YOU** for purchasing Mometrix study materials!

Second, congratulations! You are one of the few determined test-takers who are committed to doing whatever it takes to excel on your exam. **You have come to the right place.** We developed these study materials with one goal in mind: to deliver you the information you need in a format that's concise and easy to use.

In addition to optimizing your guide for the content of the test, we've outlined our recommended steps for breaking down the preparation process into small, attainable goals so you can make sure you stay on track.

We've also analyzed the entire test-taking process, identifying the most common pitfalls and showing how you can overcome them and be ready for any curveball the test throws you.

Standardized testing is one of the biggest obstacles on your road to success, which only increases the importance of doing well in the high-pressure, high-stakes environment of test day. Your results on this test could have a significant impact on your future, and this guide provides the information and practical advice to help you achieve your full potential on test day.

Your success is our success

We would love to hear from you! If you would like to share the story of your exam success or if you have any questions or comments in regard to our products, please contact us at **800-673-8175** or **support@mometrix.com**.

Thanks again for your business and we wish you continued success!

Sincerely,
The Mometrix Test Preparation Team

Need more help? Check out our flashcards at:
http://MometrixFlashcards.com/ASCS

Written and edited by the Mometrix Exam Secrets Test Prep Team
Printed in the United States of America

TABLE OF CONTENTS

Introduction

Thank you for purchasing this resource! You have made the choice to prepare yourself for a test that could have a huge impact on your future, and this guide is designed to help you be fully ready for test day. Obviously, it's important to have a solid understanding of the test material, but you also need to be prepared for the unique environment and stressors of the test, so that you can perform to the best of your abilities.

For this purpose, the first section that appears in this guide is the **Secret Keys**. We've devoted countless hours to meticulously researching what works and what doesn't, and we've boiled down our findings to the five most impactful steps you can take to improve your performance on the test. We start at the beginning with study planning and move through the preparation process, all the way to the testing strategies that will help you get the most out of what you know when you're finally sitting in front of the test.

We recommend that you start preparing for your test as far in advance as possible. However, if you've bought this guide as a last-minute study resource and only have a few days before your test, we recommend that you skip over the first two Secret Keys since they address a long-term study plan.

If you struggle with **test anxiety**, we strongly encourage you to check out our recommendations for how you can overcome it. Test anxiety is a formidable foe, but it can be beaten, and we want to make sure you have the tools you need to defeat it.

Secret Key 1: Plan Big, Study Small

There's a lot riding on your performance. If you want to ace this test, you're going to need to keep your skills sharp and the material fresh in your mind. You need a plan that lets you review everything you need to know while still fitting in your schedule. We'll break this strategy down into three categories.

Information Organization

Start with the information you already have: the official test outline. From this, you can make a complete list of all the concepts you need to cover before the test. Organize these concepts into groups that can be studied together, and create a list of any related vocabulary you need to learn so you can brush up on any difficult terms. You'll want to keep this vocabulary list handy once you actually start studying since you may need to add to it along the way.

Time Management

Once you have your set of study concepts, decide how to spread them out over the time you have left before the test. Break your study plan into small, clear goals so you have a manageable task for each day and know exactly what you're doing. Then just focus on one small step at a time. When you manage your time this way, you don't need to spend hours at a time studying. Studying a small block of content for a short period each day helps you retain information better and avoid stressing over how much you have left to do. You can relax knowing that you have a plan to cover everything in time. In order for this strategy to be effective though, you have to start studying early and stick to your schedule. Avoid the exhaustion and futility that comes from last-minute cramming!

Study Environment

The environment you study in has a big impact on your learning. Studying in a coffee shop, while probably more enjoyable, is not likely to be as fruitful as studying in a quiet room. It's important to keep distractions to a minimum. You're only planning to study for a short block of time, so make the most of it. Don't pause to check your phone or get up to find a snack. It's also important to **avoid multitasking**. Research has consistently shown that multitasking will make your studying dramatically less effective. Your study area should also be comfortable and well-lit so you don't have the distraction of straining your eyes or sitting on an uncomfortable chair.

The time of day you study is also important. You want to be rested and alert. Don't wait until just before bedtime. Study when you'll be most likely to comprehend and remember. Even better, if you know what time of day your test will be, set that time aside for study. That way your brain will be used to working on that subject at that specific time and you'll have a better chance of recalling information.

Finally, it can be helpful to team up with others who are studying for the same test. Your actual studying should be done in as isolated an environment as possible, but the work of organizing the information and setting up the study plan can be divided up. In between study sessions, you can discuss with your teammates the concepts that you're all studying and quiz each other on the details. Just be sure that your teammates are as serious about the test as you are. If you find that your study time is being replaced with social time, you might need to find a new team.

Secret Key 2: Make Your Studying Count

You're devoting a lot of time and effort to preparing for this test, so you want to be absolutely certain it will pay off. This means doing more than just reading the content and hoping you can remember it on test day. It's important to make every minute of study count. There are two main areas you can focus on to make your studying count.

Retention

It doesn't matter how much time you study if you can't remember the material. You need to make sure you are retaining the concepts. To check your retention of the information you're learning, try recalling it at later times with minimal prompting. Try carrying around flashcards and glance at one or two from time to time or ask a friend who's also studying for the test to quiz you.

To enhance your retention, look for ways to put the information into practice so that you can apply it rather than simply recalling it. If you're using the information in practical ways, it will be much easier to remember. Similarly, it helps to solidify a concept in your mind if you're not only reading it to yourself but also explaining it to someone else. Ask a friend to let you teach them about a concept you're a little shaky on (or speak aloud to an imaginary audience if necessary). As you try to summarize, define, give examples, and answer your friend's questions, you'll understand the concepts better and they will stay with you longer. Finally, step back for a big picture view and ask yourself how each piece of information fits with the whole subject. When you link the different concepts together and see them working together as a whole, it's easier to remember the individual components.

Finally, practice showing your work on any multi-step problems, even if you're just studying. Writing out each step you take to solve a problem will help solidify the process in your mind, and you'll be more likely to remember it during the test.

Modality

Modality simply refers to the means or method by which you study. Choosing a study modality that fits your own individual learning style is crucial. No two people learn best in exactly the same way, so it's important to know your strengths and use them to your advantage.

For example, if you learn best by visualization, focus on visualizing a concept in your mind and draw an image or a diagram. Try color-coding your notes, illustrating them, or creating symbols that will trigger your mind to recall a learned concept. If you learn best by hearing or discussing information, find a study partner who learns the same way or read aloud to yourself. Think about how to put the information in your own words. Imagine that you are giving a lecture on the topic and record yourself so you can listen to it later.

For any learning style, flashcards can be helpful. Organize the information so you can take advantage of spare moments to review. Underline key words or phrases. Use different colors for different categories. Mnemonic devices (such as creating a short list in which every item starts with the same letter) can also help with retention. Find what works best for you and use it to store the information in your mind most effectively and easily.

Secret Key 3: Practice the Right Way

Your success on test day depends not only on how many hours you put into preparing, but also on whether you prepared the right way. It's good to check along the way to see if your studying is paying off. One of the most effective ways to do this is by taking practice tests to evaluate your progress. Practice tests are useful because they show exactly where you need to improve. Every time you take a practice test, pay special attention to these three groups of questions:

- The questions you got wrong
- The questions you had to guess on, even if you guessed right
- The questions you found difficult or slow to work through

This will show you exactly what your weak areas are, and where you need to devote more study time. Ask yourself why each of these questions gave you trouble. Was it because you didn't understand the material? Was it because you didn't remember the vocabulary? Do you need more repetitions on this type of question to build speed and confidence? Dig into those questions and figure out how you can strengthen your weak areas as you go back to review the material.

Additionally, many practice tests have a section explaining the answer choices. It can be tempting to read the explanation and think that you now have a good understanding of the concept. However, an explanation likely only covers part of the question's broader context. Even if the explanation makes perfect sense, **go back and investigate** every concept related to the question until you're positive you have a thorough understanding.

As you go along, keep in mind that the practice test is just that: practice. Memorizing these questions and answers will not be very helpful on the actual test because it is unlikely to have any of the same exact questions. If you only know the right answers to the sample questions, you won't be prepared for the real thing. **Study the concepts** until you understand them fully, and then you'll be able to answer any question that shows up on the test.

It's important to wait on the practice tests until you're ready. If you take a test on your first day of study, you may be overwhelmed by the amount of material covered and how much you need to learn. Work up to it gradually.

On test day, you'll need to be prepared for answering questions, managing your time, and using the test-taking strategies you've learned. It's a lot to balance, like a mental marathon that will have a big impact on your future. Like training for a marathon, you'll need to start slowly and work your way up. When test day arrives, you'll be ready.

Start with the strategies you've read in the first two Secret Keys—plan your course and study in the way that works best for you. If you have time, consider using multiple study resources to get different approaches to the same concepts. It can be helpful to see difficult concepts from more than one angle. Then find a good source for practice tests. Many times, the test website will suggest potential study resources or provide sample tests.

Practice Test Strategy

If you're able to find at least three practice tests, we recommend this strategy:

Untimed and Open-Book Practice

Take the first test with no time constraints and with your notes and study guide handy. Take your time and focus on applying the strategies you've learned.

Timed and Open-Book Practice

Take the second practice test open-book as well, but set a timer and practice pacing yourself to finish in time.

Timed and Closed-Book Practice

Take any other practice tests as if it were test day. Set a timer and put away your study materials. Sit at a table or desk in a quiet room, imagine yourself at the testing center, and answer questions as quickly and accurately as possible.

Keep repeating timed and closed-book tests on a regular basis until you run out of practice tests or it's time for the actual test. Your mind will be ready for the schedule and stress of test day, and you'll be able to focus on recalling the material you've learned.

Secret Key 4: Pace Yourself

Once you're fully prepared for the material on the test, your biggest challenge on test day will be managing your time. Just knowing that the clock is ticking can make you panic even if you have plenty of time left. Work on pacing yourself so you can build confidence against the time constraints of the exam. Pacing is a difficult skill to master, especially in a high-pressure environment, so **practice is vital**.

Set time expectations for your pace based on how much time is available. For example, if a section has 60 questions and the time limit is 30 minutes, you know you have to average 30 seconds or less per question in order to answer them all. Although 30 seconds is the hard limit, set 25 seconds per question as your goal, so you reserve extra time to spend on harder questions. When you budget extra time for the harder questions, you no longer have any reason to stress when those questions take longer to answer.

Don't let this time expectation distract you from working through the test at a calm, steady pace, but keep it in mind so you don't spend too much time on any one question. Recognize that taking extra time on one question you don't understand may keep you from answering two that you do understand later in the test. If your time limit for a question is up and you're still not sure of the answer, mark it and move on, and come back to it later if the time and the test format allow. If the testing format doesn't allow you to return to earlier questions, just make an educated guess; then put it out of your mind and move on.

On the easier questions, be careful not to rush. It may seem wise to hurry through them so you have more time for the challenging ones, but it's not worth missing one if you know the concept and just didn't take the time to read the question fully. Work efficiently but make sure you understand the question and have looked at all of the answer choices, since more than one may seem right at first.

Even if you're paying attention to the time, you may find yourself a little behind at some point. You should speed up to get back on track, but do so wisely. Don't panic; just take a few seconds less on each question until you're caught up. Don't guess without thinking, but do look through the answer choices and eliminate any you know are wrong. If you can get down to two choices, it is often worthwhile to guess from those. Once you've chosen an answer, move on and don't dwell on any that you skipped or had to hurry through. If a question was taking too long, chances are it was one of the harder ones, so you weren't as likely to get it right anyway.

On the other hand, if you find yourself getting ahead of schedule, it may be beneficial to slow down a little. The more quickly you work, the more likely you are to make a careless mistake that will affect your score. You've budgeted time for each question, so don't be afraid to spend that time. Practice an efficient but careful pace to get the most out of the time you have.

Secret Key 5: Have a Plan for Guessing

When you're taking the test, you may find yourself stuck on a question. Some of the answer choices seem better than others, but you don't see the one answer choice that is obviously correct. What do you do?

The scenario described above is very common, yet most test takers have not effectively prepared for it. Developing and practicing a plan for guessing may be one of the single most effective uses of your time as you get ready for the exam.

In developing your plan for guessing, there are three questions to address:

- When should you start the guessing process?
- How should you narrow down the choices?
- Which answer should you choose?

When to Start the Guessing Process

Unless your plan for guessing is to select C every time (which, despite its merits, is not what we recommend), you need to leave yourself enough time to apply your answer elimination strategies. Since you have a limited amount of time for each question, that means that if you're going to give yourself the best shot at guessing correctly, you have to decide quickly whether or not you will guess.

Of course, the best-case scenario is that you don't have to guess at all, so first, see if you can answer the question based on your knowledge of the subject and basic reasoning skills. Focus on the key words in the question and try to jog your memory of related topics. Give yourself a chance to bring the knowledge to mind, but once you realize that you don't have (or you can't access) the knowledge you need to answer the question, it's time to start the guessing process.

It's almost always better to start the guessing process too early than too late. It only takes a few seconds to remember something and answer the question from knowledge. Carefully eliminating wrong answer choices takes longer. Plus, going through the process of eliminating answer choices can actually help jog your memory.

Summary: Start the guessing process as soon as you decide that you can't answer the question based on your knowledge.

How to Narrow Down the Choices

The next chapter in this book (**Test-Taking Strategies**) includes a wide range of strategies for how to approach questions and how to look for answer choices to eliminate. You will definitely want to read those carefully, practice them, and figure out which ones work best for you. Here though, we're going to address a mindset rather than a particular strategy.

Your odds of guessing an answer correctly depend on how many options you are choosing from.

Number of options left	5	4	3	2	1
Odds of guessing correctly	20%	25%	33%	50%	100%

You can see from this chart just how valuable it is to be able to eliminate incorrect answers and make an educated guess, but there are two things that many test takers do that cause them to miss out on the benefits of guessing:

- Accidentally eliminating the correct answer
- Selecting an answer based on an impression

We'll look at the first one here, and the second one in the next section.

To avoid accidentally eliminating the correct answer, we recommend a thought exercise called **the $5 challenge**. In this challenge, you only eliminate an answer choice from contention if you are willing to bet $5 on it being wrong. Why $5? Five dollars is a small but not insignificant amount of money. It's an amount you could afford to lose but wouldn't want to throw away. And while losing $5 once might not hurt too much, doing it twenty times will set you back $100. In the same way, each small decision you make—eliminating a choice here, guessing on a question there—won't by itself impact your score very much, but when you put them all together, they can make a big difference. By holding each answer choice elimination decision to a higher standard, you can reduce the risk of accidentally eliminating the correct answer.

The $5 challenge can also be applied in a positive sense: If you are willing to bet $5 that an answer choice *is* correct, go ahead and mark it as correct.

Summary: Only eliminate an answer choice if you are willing to bet $5 that it is wrong.

Which Answer to Choose

You're taking the test. You've run into a hard question and decided you'll have to guess. You've eliminated all the answer choices you're willing to bet $5 on. Now you have to pick an answer. Why do we even need to talk about this? Why can't you just pick whichever one you feel like when the time comes?

The answer to these questions is that if you don't come into the test with a plan, you'll rely on your impression to select an answer choice, and if you do that, you risk falling into a trap. The test writers know that everyone who takes their test will be guessing on some of the questions, so they intentionally write wrong answer choices to seem plausible. You still have to pick an answer though, and if the wrong answer choices are designed to look right, how can you ever be sure that you're not falling for their trap? The best solution we've found to this dilemma is to take the decision out of your hands entirely. Here is the process we recommend:

Once you've eliminated any choices that you are confident (willing to bet $5) are wrong, select the first remaining choice as your answer.

Whether you choose to select the first remaining choice, the second, or the last, the important thing is that you use some preselected standard. Using this approach guarantees that you will not be enticed into selecting an answer choice that looks right, because you are not basing your decision on how the answer choices look.

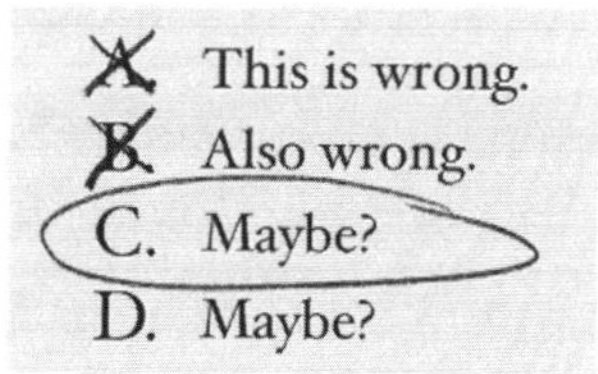

This is not meant to make you question your knowledge. Instead, it is to help you recognize the difference between your knowledge and your impressions. There's a huge difference between thinking an answer is right because of what you know, and thinking an answer is right because it looks or sounds like it should be right.

Summary: To ensure that your selection is appropriately random, make a predetermined selection from among all answer choices you have not eliminated.

Test-Taking Strategies

This section contains a list of test-taking strategies that you may find helpful as you work through the test. By taking what you know and applying logical thought, you can maximize your chances of answering any question correctly!

It is very important to realize that every question is different and every person is different: no single strategy will work on every question, and no single strategy will work for every person. That's why we've included all of them here, so you can try them out and determine which ones work best for different types of questions and which ones work best for you.

Question Strategies

✅ Read Carefully

Read the question and the answer choices carefully. Don't miss the question because you misread the terms. You have plenty of time to read each question thoroughly and make sure you understand what is being asked. Yet a happy medium must be attained, so don't waste too much time. You must read carefully and efficiently.

✅ Contextual Clues

Look for contextual clues. If the question includes a word you are not familiar with, look at the immediate context for some indication of what the word might mean. Contextual clues can often give you all the information you need to decipher the meaning of an unfamiliar word. Even if you can't determine the meaning, you may be able to narrow down the possibilities enough to make a solid guess at the answer to the question.

✅ Prefixes

If you're having trouble with a word in the question or answer choices, try dissecting it. Take advantage of every clue that the word might include. Prefixes can be a huge help. Usually, they allow you to determine a basic meaning. *Pre-* means before, *post-* means after, *pro-* is positive, *de-* is negative. From prefixes, you can get an idea of the general meaning of the word and try to put it into context.

✅ Hedge Words

Watch out for critical hedge words, such as *likely, may, can, often, almost, mostly, usually, generally, rarely*, and *sometimes*. Question writers insert these hedge phrases to cover every possibility. Often an answer choice will be wrong simply because it leaves no room for exception. Be on guard for answer choices that have definitive words such as *exactly* and *always*.

⊘ Switchback Words

Stay alert for *switchbacks*. These are the words and phrases frequently used to alert you to shifts in thought. The most common switchback words are *but*, *although*, and *however*. Others include *nevertheless*, *on the other hand*, *even though*, *while*, *in spite of*, *despite*, and *regardless of*. Switchback words are important to catch because they can change the direction of the question or an answer choice.

⊘ Face Value

When in doubt, use common sense. Accept the situation in the problem at face value. Don't read too much into it. These problems will not require you to make wild assumptions. If you have to go beyond creativity and warp time or space in order to have an answer choice fit the question, then you should move on and consider the other answer choices. These are normal problems rooted in reality. The applicable relationship or explanation may not be readily apparent, but it is there for you to figure out. Use your common sense to interpret anything that isn't clear.

Answer Choice Strategies

⊘ Answer Selection

The most thorough way to pick an answer choice is to identify and eliminate wrong answers until only one is left, then confirm it is the correct answer. Sometimes an answer choice may immediately seem right, but be careful. The test writers will usually put more than one reasonable answer choice on each question, so take a second to read all of them and make sure that the other choices are not equally obvious. As long as you have time left, it is better to read every answer choice than to pick the first one that looks right without checking the others.

⊘ Answer Choice Families

An answer choice family consists of two (in rare cases, three) answer choices that are very similar in construction and cannot all be true at the same time. If you see two answer choices that are direct opposites or parallels, one of them is usually the correct answer. For instance, if one answer choice says that quantity *x* increases and another either says that quantity *x* decreases (opposite) or says that quantity *y* increases (parallel), then those answer choices would fall into the same family. An answer choice that doesn't match the construction of the answer choice family is more likely to be incorrect. Most questions will not have answer choice families, but when they do appear, you should be prepared to recognize them.

⊘ Eliminate Answers

Eliminate answer choices as soon as you realize they are wrong, but make sure you consider all possibilities. If you are eliminating answer choices and realize that the last one you are left with is also wrong, don't panic. Start over and consider each choice again. There may be something you missed the first time that you will realize on the second pass.

✓ Avoid Fact Traps

Don't be distracted by an answer choice that is factually true but doesn't answer the question. You are looking for the choice that answers the question. Stay focused on what the question is asking for so you don't accidentally pick an answer that is true but incorrect. Always go back to the question and make sure the answer choice you've selected actually answers the question and is not merely a true statement.

✓ Extreme Statements

In general, you should avoid answers that put forth extreme actions as standard practice or proclaim controversial ideas as established fact. An answer choice that states the "process should be used in certain situations, if..." is much more likely to be correct than one that states the "process should be discontinued completely." The first is a calm rational statement and doesn't even make a definitive, uncompromising stance, using a hedge word *if* to provide wiggle room, whereas the second choice is far more extreme.

✓ Benchmark

As you read through the answer choices and you come across one that seems to answer the question well, mentally select that answer choice. This is not your final answer, but it's the one that will help you evaluate the other answer choices. The one that you selected is your benchmark or standard for judging each of the other answer choices. Every other answer choice must be compared to your benchmark. That choice is correct until proven otherwise by another answer choice beating it. If you find a better answer, then that one becomes your new benchmark. Once you've decided that no other choice answers the question as well as your benchmark, you have your final answer.

✓ Predict the Answer

Before you even start looking at the answer choices, it is often best to try to predict the answer. When you come up with the answer on your own, it is easier to avoid distractions and traps because you will know exactly what to look for. The right answer choice is unlikely to be word-for-word what you came up with, but it should be a close match. Even if you are confident that you have the right answer, you should still take the time to read each option before moving on.

General Strategies

✓ Tough Questions

If you are stumped on a problem or it appears too hard or too difficult, don't waste time. Move on! Remember though, if you can quickly check for obviously incorrect answer choices, your chances of guessing correctly are greatly improved. Before you completely give up, at least try to knock out a couple of possible answers. Eliminate what you can and then guess at the remaining answer choices before moving on.

✅ Check Your Work

Since you will probably not know every term listed and the answer to every question, it is important that you get credit for the ones that you do know. Don't miss any questions through careless mistakes. If at all possible, try to take a second to look back over your answer selection and make sure you've selected the correct answer choice and haven't made a costly careless mistake (such as marking an answer choice that you didn't mean to mark). This quick double check should more than pay for itself in caught mistakes for the time it costs.

✅ Pace Yourself

It's easy to be overwhelmed when you're looking at a page full of questions; your mind is confused and full of random thoughts, and the clock is ticking down faster than you would like. Calm down and maintain the pace that you have set for yourself. Especially as you get down to the last few minutes of the test, don't let the small numbers on the clock make you panic. As long as you are on track by monitoring your pace, you are guaranteed to have time for each question.

✅ Don't Rush

It is very easy to make errors when you are in a hurry. Maintaining a fast pace in answering questions is pointless if it makes you miss questions that you would have gotten right otherwise. Test writers like to include distracting information and wrong answers that seem right. Taking a little extra time to avoid careless mistakes can make all the difference in your test score. Find a pace that allows you to be confident in the answers that you select.

✅ Keep Moving

Panicking will not help you pass the test, so do your best to stay calm and keep moving. Taking deep breaths and going through the answer elimination steps you practiced can help to break through a stress barrier and keep your pace.

Final Notes

The combination of a solid foundation of content knowledge and the confidence that comes from practicing your plan for applying that knowledge is the key to maximizing your performance on test day. As your foundation of content knowledge is built up and strengthened, you'll find that the strategies included in this chapter become more and more effective in helping you quickly sift through the distractions and traps of the test to isolate the correct answer.

Now that you're preparing to move forward into the test content chapters of this book, be sure to keep your goal in mind. As you read, think about how you will be able to apply this information on the test. If you've already seen sample questions for the test and you have an idea of the question format and style, try to come up with questions of your own that you can answer based on what you're reading. This will give you valuable practice applying your knowledge in the same ways you can expect to on test day.

Good luck and good studying!

Sheet Metal Air Ducts

When creating an opening in a sheet metal air duct with **internal insulation**, one must first determine the size of the opening and then using a template, cut an opening into the duct approximately 2" smaller than the size of the closure panel. This ensures enough room to seal and fasten the opening to the air duct. Upon completion of the job, the closing panel should be outfitted with a duct liner glued to the inside of the panel prior to sealing the opening. If a rigid liner board was used for the interior of the duct, it may be reused provided that there are no defects present. Installing the closure panel requires applying a sealant around the opening and then attaching the closure panel with screws approximately 4" O.C. into the duct wall. A tape may also be used for sealing the opening, however, after the mechanical fasteners have been put in place.

To open a section of the sheet metal air duct that has been **externally insulated**, one must first consider whether the opening will create a permanent access door, or if the insulation will be put back in place. The reasoning for this is that the cuts into the insulation will be different as will the method used to seal the opening. If the opening is for a routine check, then the insulation needs to be cut only on three sides. The remaining side should be folded back and used later to replace the hole upon completion of the job. If the opening is to become a permanent access door, then all four sides of the insulation need to be cut and thrown away. Begin cutting into the sheet metal to create the service opening. To seal the opening upon completion of the job, a closure panel greater than 1" on all sides of the opening should be installed over the metal duct and caulking applied around the perimeter. Screws or other fasteners would be used to further secure the panel to the duct. The insulation would be folded over and fastened with staples or tape. For a permanent access door closure, the panel would not have external insulation covering the opening.

Inspections

A cleanliness inspection should be performed on every HVAC system on a routine basis according to the classification as to type of use. For example, all air-handling units should be inspected yearly regardless of whether they are used residentially, commercially, or in healthcare environments. Supply ductwork generally is checked every two years except in industrial or healthcare environments where it is checked annually. This is due to the potential for high levels of contaminants entering the system. Finally, the exhaust system should also be inspected on the same schedule as the supply ductwork. Each cleaning inspection should indicate the presence of any contaminants indicated by an increase of bacterial particles or other debris, thus indicating a need for HVAC remediation. The most common reason for a cleaning would be when construction has been performed elsewhere in the building and construction contaminants have entered the system. At this time, supply and return ductwork should also be inspected.

Air Duct Cleaning

With the advent of air conditioning, an industry has developed to insure that contaminants are removed from the air and ventilation systems. Traditionally, this was accomplished using massive suction hoses attached to a truck with brushes used to dislodge dust, dirt, and other contaminants and send them into the vacuum, thus removing them from the ventilation system. The intent was to improve the air flow through the system and allow it to work more efficiently in both the heating and cooling processes. As time progressed, better ways to clean out a HVAC (heating, ventilation, & air conditioning) infrastructure were developed and the focus shifted to improving the indoor air quality, or IAQ. Developments were made in designing a system for duct cleaning, now known as HVAC remediation that allowed for the cleaning of larger systems beyond the standard home size. Duct cleaning is a misnomer as a large amount of work is performed central to the HVAC unit or furnace. Additionally, as the HVAC systems have increased in efficiency, greater levels of technical knowledge and certifications are required to perform the job well.

Contaminants

Contaminations found during HVAC remediation can consist of mold, fungus, bacteria, plaster, construction materials, fiberglass, and even insect remains. Anything that was not designed to be present in the ventilation system is considered a contaminant. These contaminants can be in liquid, solid, or gaseous form. Some are considered dangerous in the sense that they may pose a health risk when touched or inhaled. Dependent upon the efficiency level of the filtration system, there may be a large amount of contaminants present in the HVAC system that is then circulated throughout the ductwork and into the air. The most common form of contaminant located in an HVAC system is dust, which if excessive, can lead to the development of bacteria. This, in turn, can transmit these bacterial contaminants throughout the home or through the facility. Minimal amounts of dust are not a problem and seldom warrant a thorough cleaning; however, a large accumulation does need to be addressed to avoid further debris contaminating the air quality of the facility.

With the safety of the building's occupants at top priority, the role of the contractor is to ensure the safe removal of contaminants and limit the exposure to new contaminants to the occupants during the cleaning process. Unless specifically hired as an Indoor Air Quality specialist, the cleaning contractor's job is to perform the remediation with minimal exposure or risk to the occupants. A consultant qualified in IAQ may need to be called on for additional evaluations of the facility. Specific issues to be addressed when performing a remediation include: paying particular attention to those individuals with respiratory problems, coordinating hours to work on the remediation with respect to the building's occupants, containing the debris while moving ventilator components through the facility, providing an estimate of the downtime to complete the cleaning process, and finally, ensuring that the work of the cleaning does not interfere with the normal scope of business at the facility.

Within the framework of an HVAC system, bacteria and fungi have preferred areas in which the conditions are ripe for breeding, such as areas around the humidifiers, the condensate drain pan, around the cooling coils. The accumulation of dust and other debris, combined with the moisture in the system, also contribute to the ideal conditions in which these microbes can multiply. It is not simply a matter of regulating the temperature cool enough to keep breeding to a minimum. That situation would not be ideal for maintaining the comfort level of the people inside the facility. The goal would therefore be to decrease the amount of contaminants present in the system through regular cleaning and also keeping the moisture at the proper levels. Bacteria, if left unchecked, can contribute to health problems in people susceptible to allergies and asthma and other respiratory conditions.

Contaminant Terms

Fungi: Any of the group of spore producing plants lacking in chlorophyll that consists of mold, mildew, and yeast.

Debris: Any substance found inside the HVAC system that was not designed to be a part of it.

Aerosols: Any particles in either solid or liquid form.

Biological contaminants: Viruses, pet dander, mold, mildew, fungi, pollen, and any of their by-products.

Bioaerosols: Airborne particles that are biologically based.

HVAC Remediation

After performing an initial cleaning inspection, the technician needs to be aware of certain scenarios in which to recommend a thorough cleaning. Through the visual observations, the technician notices an adverse amount of contaminants such as dust or debris accumulated throughout the HVAC system. There can also be growth of microbes present in the ductwork confirmed either visually or through other means of testing. If there can be a visual confirmation of contaminants being blown through the ductwork into a closed area, then a cleaning is also recommended. Finally, if there is a buildup of contaminants or deposits on the coils, air flow devices, etc. that can restrict the air flow or keep the unit from performing its job, then a cleaning should also be recommended. When indoor air quality is especially important as in the case of a home where a person with a compromised immune system lives, it is imperative that cleaning inspections be done more often to ensure proper indoor air quality.

If the facility uses multiple air-handling units, a random inspection should be performed covering several units to get a clear picture of the cleanliness of the HVAC system as a whole. All components of the unit should be inspected such as the filters, heating and cooling coils, condensate drip pans and drain lines, fans, and fan compartments. The supply and return ductwork is also inspected to include the reheat coils, return ducts, grilles, dampers, and other internal components. These parts of the HVAC unit are to be inspected visually. In performing this inspection, care must be taken to ensure that the inspection doesn't unnecessarily raise inordinate amounts of dust into the system that can be blown through the ductwork to other parts of the facility.

Once it has been determined that a home or facility is in need of remediation, the contractor and the client need to come to an agreement on the specific type of work to be performed as well as the estimated timeframe, costs, etc. This evaluation must include the degree to which the building's occupants will be displaced or whether they can continue work or living activities while the remediation is being done. An explanation of the type of cleaning and the methods used should also be included. A piece-by-piece evaluation of the components to be cleaned and the method for removing the contaminants from the HVAC system is given in the assessment. The plan should also include the system that will be used to protect the areas of the business or home to ensure that contaminants do not enter those areas. Building security will need to be addressed, as well as citing specific debris-removal procedures. All of these together comprise the Project Assessment broken down into three parts: a) building usage, b) HVAC contamination evaluation, and c) environmental impact assessment.

Environmental Engineering Controls

Environmental engineering control refers to the process to control contaminants from entering another portion of the facility during the cleaning process. It also involves monitoring where appropriate to limit the amount of contaminants entering the air in a facility. While the majority of contaminants found in an HVAC system are non-hazardous, it is wise to treat all related debris with caution to ensure that recontamination does not occur into occupied areas. Using controlled removal techniques, the goal is to successfully remove dust, debris, and other contaminants safely from the ventilation system to the vacuum system without allowing any to escape. Selecting the proper vacuum system will allow an efficient transfer of contaminants from the ductwork into the receptacle. The type of vacuum system used will also determine the length of duct that can be cleaned efficiently. The collection device must also be situated in such a way as to not re-contaminate the indoor air, nor to expel the debris into the outside air. A HEPA filter is recommended if the collection receptacle is used indoors.

Protecting Furnishings

The contractor's job involves the safe removal of contaminates from the HVAC system. This includes maintaining the IAQ of the residence or facility. Great care must be taken to prevent contaminants from landing on existing furniture, floors, and computer equipment. Prior to beginning the cleaning, occupants must be aware that their areas and spaces will be covered with a protective covering and to ensure personal articles are removed. For easier access to the workspace, furniture may need to be moved. With the portability of duct cleaning systems, equipment may be moved throughout the facility. Any type of flooring must also be well protected prior to the onset of the cleaning. It must be agreed to in advance on the amount of cleaning to be done after HVAC remediation has been completed. With the high sensitivity of electronic equipment to dust, it is imperative to provide protective coverings over the equipment if it cannot be moved. However, clearing it from the workspace is the best scenario.

Security Concerns

Any disruption to the normal business work schedule involves notification of the facility security team as well as a review of the fire safety procedures. In performing the duct cleaning, it is common for the fire alarm system in the HVAC system to be disconnected to prevent false alarms. After the cleaning has been performed, the contractor must ensure that the fire detection system has been reconnected and is working properly. Additionally, much of the work of remediation can be performed after hours and access to the facility would need to be coordinated with the security team. Doors and windows may need to remain open, and workers may be conducting the cleaning after hours. Notification of the remediation schedule to the alarm monitoring service, local fire departments, and facility management and workers will help in ensuring minimal disruption to the facility in general.

Equipment and Tools

The largest piece of cleaning equipment used in HVAC remediation consists of the vacuum collection device that is designed to collect the debris and particulate matter that was loosened in the initial brushing and scrubbing. This device also contains the matter from spreading throughout the remainder of the facility while the vacuum process is taking place. If the vacuum containment unit is exhausted indoors, it must utilize HEPA filtration with a DOP test number. The vacuum unit can either be mounted onto a truck or may be portable, allowing it to be brought into the facility. The truck-mounted unit does tend to have stronger suction power, however. Air compressors are also used to power pneumatic air tools that help with the cleaning. Hand held vacuums and wet/dry vacuums are also a common sight during a cleaning. HEPA filtration is not used with a wet vacuum, but these devices are useful for removing contaminants around condenser coils and cleaning up sludge in the drainage pan.

The common types of tools used in performing HVAC remediation can be broken down into three groups: access tools, inspection tools, and hand cleaning tools. Access tools are anything that assists in creating points of entry into the unit or ductwork. Inspection tools that help determine the extent of the debris or contaminants, which are in the system, can include a mirror, closed circuit TV, a periscope, a camera, or borescope. Hand cleaning tools can be wire or plastic bristled manual brushes, a rotary brush, scrapers, or pneumatic tools such as an air gun or blowgun. Utilizing these manual or electric brushes, the contractor then loosens the debris and particulate matter that has accumulated in the ductwork or on the unit. The pressurized air would then force these loose particles into the vacuum container to then be hauled away from the premises.

Cleaning Considerations

When using brushes to clean ductwork, the contractor must note the material in which the ductwork is made of as that has an effect on whether to use plastic or metal bristled brushes. If the material is made of metal and does not have a liner, then a brass brush would suffice, however, if fiberglass material is present, then it is more suitable to use one with softer bristles. There are no set standards to follow in determining the specific use of the equipment but an experienced contractor would have knowledge of the proper brush to use. Compressed air washing can be useful in some applications, but if the size and weight of the debris is too much, either higher agitation is necessary or another removal method must be used. Hand washing is utilized when a lighter touch is necessary or when cleaning sensitive components. Hand vacuuming can be useful when cleaning smaller spaces and when the attached brushes and hoses are sufficient in cleaning the area.

Safety Concerns

In 1970, the Occupational Safety and Health Administration enacted a series of provisions for workplace safety to ensure that proper procedures are followed to create minimal risk factors for employee injury while on the job. Prior to beginning a cleaning, the contractor should investigate whether confined spaces are present and whether a confined spaces permit is required at the facility. Hazardous chemicals are used in the remediation process therefore contractors should be aware of the risks involved from handling and using the chemicals. OSHA has designed a publication to educate workers about the risks and safety precautions of working around chemicals. Referring to the SDS (Safety Data Sheets) when working with unfamiliar substances is also advised. Lockout/tagout standard also is used to prevent accidents from the release of stored up energy while servicing a unit. Respiratory protection is mandatory in all aspects of remediation from the cleaning inspection through to the final clean up of the worksite. Particulate matter can be dislodged during any portion of the remediation and therefore poses a health risk to the contractor. Finally, personal protective equipment and regular safety training helps to minimize any further risks to the contractor.

Review Video: Intro to OSHA
Visit mometrix.com/academy and enter code: 913559

Cleaning Methodology

The right cleaning procedure depends on several factors. In certain parts of the country, high humidity plays a role in how often cleaning needs to be performed as well as the best method used to conduct the actual cleaning. High humidity produces more microbial contaminants versus dust. Due to the wide variety of cleaning equipment available, there is no best method to follow in performing the cleaning. The guidelines outlined in the NADCA Standard ACR should be adhered to with attention paid to completing the cleanliness verification. This verification consists of three parts: visual inspection, surface comparison testing, and the NADCA vacuum test. This cleanliness verification is best performed by an independent third party, at times by the client himself, but never should be conducted by the contractor doing the actual cleaning. This could result in a conflict of interest as the inspection of the work rated by the person who was hired to do it.

There are several types of cleaning methodologies:

- Vacuum Collection: Utilizing suction power and a containment receptacle to loosen debris and force the particulate matter into a collection device.
- Brushing: The cleaning contractor utilizes manual or power brushes to loosen debris within the system.
- Compressed air washing: The cleaning contractor uses a device which forces air into the duct work causing the debris to be removed from the system.
- Hand vacuuming: Also referred to as contact vacuuming, the contractor uses a canister vacuum with brush and hose attachments to physically remove the debris from inside the ductwork. This vacuum is used to clean condenser coils and if a wet vac, can also pick up sludge. These vacuums must have HEPA filtration.
- Hand washing: Using cloths, sponges, or brushes, the contractor cleans parts of the HVAC system by hand.
- Power washing: Using a wet power sprayer, the contractor cleans off certain portions of the system that will not be adversely affected by the liquid. This includes cooling and reheating coils, condensate drain pans, grilles, some types of filters, and also evaporator coils.

Points of Access

Access to a ventilation system can be obtained in many ways: through the vents, grilles, and through the ends of the ductwork. In order to reach all parts of the unit, access doors are sometimes built into the system at convenient points throughout. Occasionally it is necessary for the contractor to create an opening to facilitate the inspection or cleaning process of the HVAC system. Oftentimes, the management in the facility may express concern over the integrity of the system when the contractor needs to create an access opening. It is critical to ensure that the opening is created according to industry standards. Any openings must be airtight and provide unrestricted airflow within the system. They must also be well insulated to prevent the escape of heat or cold air. It is not recommended to create an opening in ductwork, but to simply remove the end cap at the end of the duct to gain access inside. Finally, access doors should be put at where future access may be necessary. This can include near condenser coils, dampers, near smoke detectors, and other areas that frequently need servicing.

Vacuum Device Selection

With the vacuum device being the most commonly used piece of equipment in remediation, several points must be considered in selecting the correct type. First, is it possible to bring the vacuum device into the facility and second, if so, will there be adequate means to exhaust the air. Determine where and in what manner the debris will be collected. If needed, is there HEPA filtration on the vacuum device?

Also, determine if the vacuum device rated for the proper air velocity, pressure, and air flow in order to properly complete the job. The contractor should also be aware of the location of the vacuum device during off hours, as well as the schedule for maintenance and service of the actual device. The contractor should make sure that the unit has been approved for use by NADCA and complies with industry standards. The device must be properly maintained because a poor one has the ability to decrease the IAQ of the facility and cause possible cross contamination. The size of the ductwork and the HVAC system to be cleaned determine the air velocity needed to dislodge particulate matter and send it to the collection device.

Power Wash Systems

Power washing can be inherently dangerous due to the fact that water is directed at a specific area at high velocity and can cause damage to the unit or to an individual. All contractors are required to wear safety goggles and personal protective gear and should make note if the equipment has GFCI (ground fault circuit interruption) protection. Additionally, the contractor needs to be aware of the potential for water damage from improperly using the power wash system and to prevent contaminants from washing into other areas, especially those that house building occupants. Contact with fibrous glass material is also restricted as it can cause permanent damage. The contractor must also determine the best method for disposing of the collected wastewater and whether it has the potential to damage public sewage systems and seek out a water quality specialist if needed. Determining if power washing is necessary will be done during the cleaning inspection and the client can be made aware of this as a potential cleaning method prior to beginning the job.

Surface Treatment

A surface treatment is any treatment applied to the internal ductwork of an HVAC system. Generally made of chemicals that are designed to protect the surface from microbial contaminants, they also provide a protective coating to repair internal damage. The two types of surface treatments are anti-microbial treatments and coatings and insulation repair products. Anti-microbial products are designed to prevent the growth of contaminants inside the HVAC system. It is important that they conform to EPA regulations and are rated safe for use in an HVAC system. These can be either sanitizers or disinfectants. At this time, these types of surface treatments are only rated for use on hard non-porous material. A second type of surface treatment is any product used in insulation repair. These coatings are used to repair damaged components of the HVAC system. Care must be made to ensure proper installation that will then extend the life of system components such as fibrous glass surfaces.

ACR Covers

Cleaning involves the removal of contaminants from the system whereas restoration involves some degree of repair work to be performed in order to bring the system back to its highest capacity. The standard defines how the cleaning process should take place and the proper tools to execute the job. It also covers how to determine which methodology works best in a particular scenario. Other parts of the ACR deal with biological contaminants and how to best remove them from the HVAC system. Also, a detailed outline of the cleaning of fiberglass insulation is included. Guidelines for creating access doors and service openings in ductwork and the unit itself are mentioned. Safety concerns are addressed in other parts of the standard. The ACR also discusses pre and post assessments in remediation as well as engineering concerns to be brought up in designing the cleaning procedures.

NADCA's ACR Standard

The NADCA (National Air Duct Cleaners Association) adopted a standard in 2002 called the ACR, or Assessment, Cleaning, and Restoration of HVAC systems. Adherence to this standard is a requirement for all NADCA members. In the standard, information is provided such as the guidelines to follow to ensure that the proper procedures for cleaning and restoring a HVAC system, and also to verify that the right levels of cleanliness is obtained. The ACR standard also identifies the inspection schedule to follow based on the use of a facility, whether residential or for business purposes. It also lists when certain components of the HVAC system should be cleaned and what sort of contaminants may be found in that specific area. Additionally, the Standard ACR provides guidelines in which to follow that show how best to control the possible cross-contamination while cleaning a system.

Cleaning Terms

Duct Access Door: A piece of metal through which the contractor can access the internal parts of the HVAC system. The access door can be either a permanent or temporary installation. Guidelines for creating the access door, and making a permanent closure if necessary, can be found in Standard ACR.

Flush Mount: Refers to an access door that is designed to close evenly, or flush, with the actual duct paneling.

Surface Mount: Refers to an access door or frame that extends out on top of the surface of the duct paneling.

Hinged: Having the access door and door frame attached by use of a hinge.

Sandwich: Closure of the access panel from both the interior and exterior of the duct wall.

Spin Door: A circular access door that spins inside the doorframe.

Air Duct: The passageway through which either heated or cooled air passes through and expelling out through vents and grilles.

Air Duct Covering: A covering made of fiberboard, paper, metal, or insulation that is used to cover the external portion of the air duct.

Air Duct Lining: A covering that is usually composed of fiber glass material that is used to provide internal soundproofing and thermal insulation inside the ductwork.

Double Wall Duct: A sheet metal duct that contains an inner layer of fibrous glass material covered by perforated plastic.

Ventilation

Ventilation is the process by which fresh air is circulated into a building through the use of blowers and ducts. It is generally filtered to remove contaminants prior to being expelled throughout a building. Fiber glass, fabric, and electrostatic filters can be used to filter the air. Charcoal based filters are also an option in particular when windows cannot be opened and the interior air is often recirculated, as is the case with large office buildings. Manufacturing facilities that process chemicals, paints, etc., produce dangerous fumes. Before these facilities can disperse the air from the interior, they are required by law to filter the air prior to releasing it into the environment in order keep outside contamination to a minimum. Environmental engineers help with the design of HVAC systems to ensure that pollutants are kept to a minimum while increasing the indoor air quality of our homes and businesses.

All air conditioning units that push out air can cool the air itself simply by the air movement that in turn creates a cooling sensation. However, all air conditioning units require ventilation in order to cool large amounts of air to make a difference in the room's temperature and in the comfort level of the occupants. Using forced circulation, the unit can cool down entire facilities through the use of fans located within the framework of the ducts. A propeller type fan is not strong enough to force the colder air through the ductwork into the various rooms of a home or facility. In order for the cooled air to reach all the way to the grills in each room, a centrifugal fan is most commonly used. This type of fan uses a rotating cylinder mounted inside housing similar to a spiral shape which then draws the air in and forces it down the ductwork, thus concentrating the cooled air towards the building's occupants.

The Cooling Process

Air, blowing through coiled tubing passing over a cold liquid, thus creating colder air. The liquid in the tubing is cooled through refrigeration that utilizes mechanical compressors to quickly compress and expand the liquid allowing the temperature of the fluid to decrease. Taking warm air, the liquid compresses and then, when the fluid expands, the air cools again with the warmer air then released to the outside. The cooler air is vented to the interior of the building. When the compressor uses a piston in a cylinder, it is referred to as a reciprocating compressor. Some refrigeration units alternate between liquid and gaseous substances that allow for a greater degree of cooler air to be produced and thus, cool a larger square footage of a facility. The more efficiently a unit can transfer the warmer air to the outside, the more efficient the air conditioner has become.

Air Conditioning

Air conditioning refers to the use of a mechanical system that allows for climate control within an indoor facility. Using a series of heating and cooling condensers, and ductwork through which the forced air travels, it can alter the temperature in an enclosed space such as homes, businesses, warehouses, vehicles, and airplanes.

Air conditioning can also help with humidity control, cleaning of the air, and through the filtration system, make the air less likely to house bacteria and fungi. Through the use of the air conditioner, people can exist in all types of climates. Research has shown that for optimum comfort, a temperature range of 71 degrees Fahrenheit at 70% humidity to 83 degrees Fahrenheit and 30 % humidity is the ideal comfort zone. Additionally, taking into account the ideal air velocity at 15-35 feet per minute.

Filters

Using many different types of filter, the air that is pushed through the air conditioning unit gradually is being cleaned of most contaminants prior to being expelled through the grilles and vents. Three different types of air filters are commonly used: impingement, dry, and electronic. Impingement filters are generally made of a fiberglass material coated in an adhesive that is designed to attract small particles and trap them before they are pushed further into the HVAC system. These filters have a regular schedule by which they should be replaced as they become so overwhelmed with contaminants that they cease to be as effective. A dry filter generally is shaped like an accordion. As the name indicates, these do not have an adhesive, but the glass fibers, cellulose, or synthetic fibers that make up the filter are packed in closely together to trap contaminants within. These also should be regularly changed out with new filters. Finally, electronic filters have been ionized to attract dirt and particulate matter. These do not have to be tossed out, but can be cleaned, recharged, and then replaced as necessary.

Air-Cooled vs. Water-Cooled Compressors

Generally a smaller air conditioning unit uses coiled tubing to transfer warmer air from the unit to the outside. These are referred to as air-cooled condensers. Another type known as water-cooled condensers uses water flowing through the tubing to gather heat from the unit. The water can either be cooled in a manner similar to that of an automobile radiator or it can be cooled through the evaporative process. In the evaporative method, this water then travels to a large collection area known as a cooling tower where it is then released into the air as a fine mist spray. Fresh water should be added to the cooling tower to assist with replacing the water lost during this process. These cooling towers are more commonly used in large facilities such as a factory or large office building.

Humidification/Dehumidification

Humidifying is the process by which moisture is put into the air through various means. These can be through injecting steam, spraying water into the air, or from water evaporation from heated pans. Adding moisture to the air makes the environment more comfortable for the occupants. However, too much moisture in the air can slow down perspiration in people and cause them to feel warmer than normal. In the air conditioning system, the coils generally hold much moisture, however, too much and the system overloads cause condensation to develop along the coils. This is called condensation dehumidification and is used most often in air conditioning. Finally, adsorbent dehumidification involves a layer of silica gel that picks up moisture from the air. As the gel picks up moisture from the air, it then generates heat. The cooling process of the air conditioning removes that heat and when the silica gel is fully saturated, the gel pad is then heated to remove the excess water and then reused.

Generating Heat

Heat is generated through energy processes that contribute colder air to a building or facility. Some companies even harness the heat to use during the colder months to help with lowering energy costs. The principal behind creating heat is to blow air over coils that contain hot water or steam and then force that air through the ductwork. Another method is to collect the heat made from passing electricity through metal wires and plates. Heat can be generated from refrigeration condensers, the occupants of the building themselves, and also from various lights and machines. With the rise in energy costs, more companies are forced to find alternative cost cutting measures yet still maintain proper temperature within their own facilities. Using the heat generated from these sources, the warm air is vented out from a room into a heat exchanger, which then transfers the heat into another form such as water. The water is then repurposed back into the facility and the expended cold air is released outside. This method saves on energy and fuel costs.

Air Conditioning Unit Types

A common household air conditioning window unit is known as a self-contained air conditioner, simply defined because all the parts necessary to run it are contained within its four walls. Modern homes have central a/c which is defined as having the mechanisms in one area, the controls in yet another, and the ductwork spread throughout the house or facility. Environmental control systems are more complicated and one would find them in a larger facility such as a corporation or a hospital. Often computerized, these systems are capable of several functions in many locations onsite. Additionally, types of air conditioning units can be broken down according to the specifics of how they work. For example, these units can be a refrigeration compressor, a heat pump, steam jet, or air cycle.

Refrigeration compressor units utilize a reciprocating compressor, which then cools the air by compressing, then expanding the fluid in an enclosed tube and blowing air over the coils to then create the cooler air. The warmer air is then expelled outside. A **heat pump unit** reverses the process by which heat is transferred from one area to another and thus cooling can occur. However, the heat pump is designed to take warm air and then increase its temperature before expending back inside. Steam-jet coolers are designed for use in large facilities only. They work by vaporizing water at low temperatures in a vacuum and then injecting it with steam at a high temperature. **Steam-jet units** work well with systems that use a boiler for heating. An **air-cycle unit** cools by using air to cool air. Generally these are used in high-speed aircraft where a tube compresses the air that is forced into it and the air itself does not liquefy.

Used in most single-family homes and in large businesses, **central heating** is designed to distribute heat throughout a home or facility in an even manner. The heat dispersed in central heating comes from burning fuel in a furnace, from heating water into steam, or it can come from heating recirculated room air. This heating can come from the same unit that provides cooling air during the summer. A hot water system heats the liquid in a furnace and then it travels through insulated pipes and finally expelled through radiator placed in various rooms in a building. The colder air is returned through pipes back to the furnace for recirculation. When cold air reaches the radiator pipes, the hot air rises and circulates throughout the room. Valves are located on the radiator to control the amount of heat put out into the room. Additionally, hot water pipes may be laid in concrete floors as another method of hot water heating in which these pipes heat the floor by conduction and the air in the room by radiation.

Furnaces

A furnace is a simple structure made of two basic parts: the area where fuel is burned, also known as the combustion chamber, and the heat exchanger, where the transfer of the heat is made to another medium such as water, air, or steam. Traditionally, burning coal was used to create the heat, but today, cleaner burning fuels such as fuel oil and natural gas area used. In remote locations or in homes not used year-round, propane is also an option. Furnaces are designed with automatic shut-off protection in the event the temperature exceeds a designated level. Gas furnaces generally have an efficiency rating of around 70-80% meaning that this percentage is the amount of the heating energy is returned into the home. Oil furnaces are rated in the 60% range and are not as efficient, unless the furnace has had regular cleaning and maintenance.

Hot-Air Systems

Originating from a furnace, the hot air travels through a series of pipes to registers located on the floor of rooms of a home or business. These registers have dampers that allow an individual to control the amount of heat that comes into the room. As the hot air flows into the room, it rises and circulates around. Located a distance away from the inlet register, the return ducts take the colder air and send it back in the direction of the furnace to start the process over again. This method is an inexpensive manner of heating an area and it works well with a central air conditioning system, however, if the same system is used for cooling, additional ductwork and registers need to be installed.

Thermostats

Most home heating systems have one thermostat while large buildings and facilities may be zoned and therefore have multiple thermostats specific to each location. In a standard thermostat, a desired temperature is entered into the system. If the temperature in the room gets higher than what was programmed, the system kicks in causing the unit to generate cooler air. A similar process takes place when heating a room. A primary element located inside the thermostat is responsible for initiating the desired heating or cooling action. When the temperature surpasses the desired number, then the element expands or contracts along with the room's temperature. This primary element then activates an electrical switch that in turn activates the secondary element that regulates the temperature. Some primary elements contain mercury in a flexible tube that as the temperature increases or decreases beyond the desired state, the tube then makes the contact with wires at one end completing a circuit and thus initiating the heating or cooling.

High-Efficiency Furnaces

The newer gas fired high efficiency furnaces can boast ratings of around 93-97% efficiency. The main criterion is that there is an increased surface area on the heat exchanger which then forces air all around the house. These furnaces do not use a pilot light to initiate combustion, but rather rely upon a spark plug. Additionally, these furnaces use the air from outside rather than the indoor air to aid in combustion. In pulsed combustion, air and gas are combined in a combustion compartment and then as pressure valves for both the gas and air are closed, the mixture is forced through the pipes into the heat exchanger area. This pulsating action completes its cycle at approximately 60-70 times per second, each time regenerating new air into the system.

Electric Radiant Heating

Radiant heating consists of electric resistance heaters laid into a concrete floor, which then generates heat through conduction, radiation and convection. This method of heating is generally more expensive and therefore is mostly used in parts of the country that have shorter winters, usually in the South. It does provide more comfortable temperatures and the time to heat a room is faster than other methods. The output temperature of radiant heating is higher than that of a heat pump. A heat pump does have a slower heating time and is also more costly than traditional heating methods. A heat pump works by taking air from the ground or the air and releases it into the building. This method also works best in a moderate climate as the amount of energy expended through this method is less than that required by mechanical or electrical means. However, heat pumps also require an auxiliary method of heating when the outside temperature drops too low.

Solar Power

When designing a solar heating system, you need to have several items in place: a glass collector panel, water or air distribution system, and a storage container. The glass panel should be installed on the roof of the building at a steep angle and facing southward. The water or air distribution system consists of multiple tubes under a heat absorption pad that then heats the water or air as the sun's rays hit the outer glass. Finally, a storage tank holds the heated water or air and then sends this off to the heat exchanger where the warm air is then processed throughout the rest of the building. To heat the home, the hot water or air can be taken directly from the collection system or from the storage tank. Although solar power is an energy efficient means by which to heat a home or building, one must still rely on standard heating processes such as a furnace.

Stoves, Fireplaces, and Space Heaters

Wood stoves are more commonly used in rural parts of the country when energy costs are high and the costs of firewood are considerably lower. There is the potential for a house fire when using wood stoves and also the possibility of carbon monoxide poisoning. Fireplaces are used to also heat homes and can be quite cost effective; however, the range in which they heat a room is limited to the immediate vicinity of the fireplace. Air from the rest of the room is utilized in order to create the fire and the expended air is minimal by contrast. To correct this, modifications are made to the area around the fireplace such as adding separate ducts on either side of the fireplace which draw air into it, allowing the air to be heated, and then releasing the warmed air back into the room. Space heaters are designed to heat a single room or small area only. To create the heat, electric passes through resistance elements which then become red-hot. A reflective surface at the back of the heater pushes the warmed air out into the room. Space heaters need extra vigilance as they can be a fire hazard if clothing, drapes or other material gets too close to the heating elements.

Energy Efficient Cooling Systems

With higher energy costs beginning in the 1970 many manufacturers began to look for better ways of making the standard units more efficient and better able to produce heating and cooling at a lower cost. The EER, or energy efficiency ratio, is defined as the amount of cooling a unit is able to produce in comparison to the total cost to operate the unit. The higher the number, the more efficient that unit is. A good number when researching units should be 10.0 and up. Although the exact cost of the unit may be higher, it can result in a cost savings in energy spending over the long run. Another factor that can help with the unit's efficiency is in selecting the correct size unit for its intended use. A unit designed for a large facility will result in higher humidity levels and the consumption of more energy than necessary. By contrast, a unit that is too small may produce smaller amounts of humidity and will not cool the air sufficiently. It is imperative to determine the cooling load for a particular facility by taking into account the size and shape of the space as well as the identifying the number of people who will likely occupy the space.

Efficiency

An engineer can be consulted to determine the best methods for increasing efficiency without installing an entirely new system. Performing a complete inspection, replacing worn out components, and putting the unit on a regular maintenance schedule can increase its output while not costing the client much. The engineer could also review the original design of the unit to see if any structural changes were made that are detrimental to its performance. Reducing the resistance in airflow throughout the system can also help it run more efficiently as can turning down the system so that it does not work as hard to either heat or cool. Switching to a control system that allows for temperature and zone control can help prevent unwanted heating and cooling of areas which are not regularly in use. Finally, using a VAV or variable air volume system enables the air conditioning unit to control the quantity of air into a particular area while not creating a reduction in temperature. Engineers generally recommend this method where zoned air is a client requirement.

Relative Humidity

Relative humidity is defined as the percentage of moisture in the air with relation to the amount of moisture that the air is able to hold at a given temperature. The range at which a person is most comfortable is with the relative humidity anywhere between 30-70%. Because cold air does not retain as much moisture as warmer air, the winter season tends to produce dryer conditions. Most central air units have a humidifier built into the furnace; however, steam and water systems require a separate room humidifier. To assist in determine the average fuel consumption for a region, a calculation known as "degree days" can be used. With heating generally necessitated at anything 65 degrees and below, any average daily temperature below that number constitutes one degree day. This calculation can give a rough estimate of the amount of fuel that would be consumed in the season. You would also need to factor in the relative temperature of the home or building.

Insulation

Although most homes are built with sufficient insulation in the walls and attics, the majority of heat loss occurs near windows and doors. Double paned windows create an insulation of air in between two panes of glass which helps to keep out heat loss. During the winter, one can also use heavy drapery to maintain heat within the home. Some companies even have developed an adhesive paper that would reflect the heat back into the home. Additionally, proper caulking and weather stripping around doors and windows create another barrier. Insulation in the walls generally is between 2-3 inches deep and in the attic can be up to 6 inches deep. Although maintaining insulation in the home is important for heat retention, it is equally important not to seal the home entirely and to allow for fresh air to enter the home. Ventilation may be advised in cases like these.

Single-Zone vs. Multi-Zone HVAC Units

A single-zone unit relies upon one thermostat to control the temperature in a facility. This thermostat can only control the temperature within one building that has a single unit for transmitting heating and cooling throughout the building. The downside to this system is that there is a tendency for variances in temperature from room to room, which can then cause comfort issues for the occupants. Additionally, the temperature in building areas that have higher solar exposure due to poor insulation or large windows may fluctuate in response to the radiant heat from the sun. In a multi-zoned unit, variances in temperature can be achieved through controls that are specific to an area. Adjustments can be made to increase the comfort level of building occupants. Cooler rooms can be made in areas where equipment such as computers and copiers put out heat from their use, and also depending on the amount of sun an area gets, the temperature controls can adjust to make the room feel cooler than it normally would.

Important Titles

System Operator: The system operator is responsible for knowing the mechanics of the HVAC system and how it works within the facility. This person should also ensure that the unit is inspected and cleaned on a regular basis. The system operator is also entrusted with maintaining the temperature within of the facility to keep the occupants at a comfortable level. This person is usually the first point of contact for any issues regarding the HVAC unit.

Facility Manager: The facility manager is responsible for keeping the system current and serves as the person who makes the financial decisions on whether to repair the unit or completely replace it.

Indoor Air Quality Specialist: The IAQ specialist generally serves as a consultant. This person has a background in HVAC remediation, has experience in identifying the types of contaminants normally found in these units, and can present a plan for reducing the number of contaminants in the inside air of a facility. This, in turn, improves the air quality and lowers the health risks for individuals with respiratory concerns.

Testing and Balancing

The purpose of the test and balance is to ensure that the HVAC system is operating at its greatest capacity and in the most efficient manner. When the unit is newly installed, the system should undergo a test and balance to provide a benchmark against which all further measurements can be compared. Testing and balancing involves checking all components of the HVAC system to ensure they are working properly. Testing ensures that the operating costs of the unit are kept down and that the unit would have an extended life due to being properly maintained. The original design of the HVAC system should be kept on record and used as a guideline when testing the following features: the control settings and the basic operation of the unit, the air flow, air temperature, the rate in the supply, return, exhaust, and outdoor airflow, the filtration system and how well it attracts contaminants, the speed of the fans and how much power the actual unit uses. The person contracted for testing and balancing the system should be an independent third party who can provide an unbiased report.

The contractor hired to perform the test and balance is looking for several concerns. This person needs to ensure that the operation of the HVAC unit is in compliance with its design specifications. These specs are generally available from the building owner. The contractor also needs to seek out and identify any problems with the system. Finally, any safety concerns involved with system operations need to be identified. In determining whether a system should be tested and balanced, several guidelines can be followed. Anytime construction has been made to a facility resulting in greater occupancy and additional square footage being added, the system should be evaluated to see if it is capable of meeting an increased workload. If occupant complaints are on the increase and if any modifications have been made to the system, then a testing is warranted. Finally, testing and balancing should be done if original documentation cannot be located to ensure compliance with indoor air quality and with the original design specifications.

Constant Volume vs. Variable Volume

In a system that utilizes constant volume airflow, the air flowing out of the grilles regulates the temperature of the room. The unit will shut off the airflow periodically when the temperature has reached a preset level. This system works with both heating and cooling the air. By contrast, a variable volume system maintains the temperature level through the use of increasing or decreasing the volume of the heated or cooled air being blown into a particular area. These types of systems also will allow the user to control the temperature of the air in response to seasonal needs. There is the potential with both scenarios to overheat or overcool an area if the systems are not adjusted to reflect changes in temperature. Variable air volume systems also need to have adequate ventilation of outside air periodically or under ventilation may occur.

HVAC Components

The basic components that make up a HVAC system are:

- Ductwork
- Heating and cooling coils
- Condensate drip pans
- Air filters
- Humidifier
- Outdoor air control
- Supply fan
- Temperature control panel
- Outside intake
- Return air system
- Exhaust fan
- Boiler
- Cooling tower

Mixed-Air Plenums

A plenum is a space that serves as a receiving point in which outside air combines with return air to either heat or cool the building. Once the outdoor air damper is opened, it combines with the air that has been circulated already through the HVAC system and is then put back into circulation throughout the facility. If the dampers are not opened to the proper level, too much air can enter the plenum causing changes in temperature and requiring further adjustments. The dampers can be controlled to fluctuate the size of the openings in response to the temperature of the outdoors, or to address the needs of the building's ventilation and exhaust. When outdoor temperatures are at extreme highs or lows, the dampers open only minimal amounts. As the air outside gets closer to the desired temperature indoors, the dampers open wider allowing more external air to be mixed in the plenum rather than using larger portions of the return air.

Outdoor Air Intake

An outdoor air intake is the structure, generally situated on the roof of a building or facility, which draws in air to be used to heat or cool the interior of the building. The model of the intake can vary depending on the size of the unit and also the type of unit that ultimately provides interior temperature control. The location of the unit on the top of the building should receive special consideration as the potential to introduce harm to the interior can occur if the intake is situated too close to exhaust that releases pollutants into the air. Additionally, the intake should have safeguards in place to prevent debris such as leaves, stones, precipitation, and even small animals from entering the intake. These all have the potential to contaminate the air drawn into the HVAC unit. If too much air is exhausted out versus that which comes in through the intake, a scenario may develop in which air enters through the facility through leakage sites.

Freezestats

A freezestat is simply a device that regulates the opening of the damper in response to changes in the temperature. If the temperature falls below a preset number, then the freezestat takes over and eliminates the possibility for outside air to be brought into the system. At its basic level, it is a temperature control device that is designed to protect the coils in the event of a temperature fluctuation. This is commonly found in many HVAC designs today. If a freezestat is "tripped" and is not reset, then inadequate ventilation becomes a problem. At times, if there is a great variance in the temperature of the outside air and the temperature of the return air, the system may also "trip" and need to be reset. One solution would be to adjust the size of the damper opening, however, that may reduce the amount of outside air being drawn into the system and thus, dispersed throughout the facility.

Air Economizer Cooling Systems

An air economizer system is one that uses the outside air to regulate the temperature inside a building. The controller takes in outside air and mixes it with indoor air to create air that registers between 55-65 degrees. Once the air is cooled to this temperature range, it is then further heated or cooled to the desired temperature for the building occupants. Air economizer systems also have a mechanism that controls the degree to which the outside dampers are opened or closed. The goal is to provide the maximum in ventilation while also decreasing the amount of energy being put out to provide the heating or cooling. Additionally, if there is balance in the system between the outdoor air make-up and the exhaust and the zone temperature controls are functioning well, then it is possible to measure the minimum amount of outdoor airflow and compare it to the ventilation standards. To gather this information it will be necessary to measure the air flow at the outside intake and also take a reading of the percentage of outdoor air within the system. The amount of CO_2 in an enclosed space will also determine the extent to which the system is ventilating properly. Another method is to use tracer gases to determine ventilation and airflow patterns.

Supply Fans

All homes and businesses generate dust and dirt from day to day activities. As such, minimal amounts are considered normal in the HVAC unit. Dust and dirt can affect many components of the HVAC system from coils, ductwork, to the housing and can redistribute this dust back into the air. When the dust and dirt is excessive, problems arise in which the buildup of dust in the ductwork causes the unit to run less efficiently, using more power to provide the same amount of cooling or heating as before, and can contribute to a host of health problems that arise from breathing contaminated air. In order to reduce the potential for this problem becoming more serious, regular cleaning of the home or facility is necessary to remove excessive dust. Additionally, cleaning of the drain pans, inspecting for leaks in the system, and making any necessary repairs due to water damage will ensure that further contamination does not occur.

Exhaust Fans

Exhaust fans are required by building codes to remove air from areas that have a high propensity for introducing contaminants back into the air. These areas can include kitchens, bathrooms, paint shops, chemistry labs, etc., where the air can be filled with hazardous fumes or gases. Exhausting the air from one location causes negative pressure to build up and therefore, the design of the HVAC system should take this into consideration by ensuring that appropriate amounts of outside air be brought into the facility to stabilize this negative pressure. The make-up air must primarily be sent to the area that is being exhausted. By design, the exhaust system should not be connected to the main HVAC system to avoid cross contamination. If there is any excess make-up air drawn in, it is then expelled through the relief outlets. When a positive or neutral environment is created with regards to air pressure, it then decreases the amount of soil gases that could contaminate the air. To achieve a positive pressured environment, the building must be tightly constructed.

Terminal Devices

A terminal device is any mechanism such as an exhaust grille, return grille, damper, control, etc. that allows for the distribution of air within a set space. Generally, these terminal devices are located near the ceilings or on the floors in older homes. The location of the terminal devices is important because that influences the degree to which air properly covers the room and changes the temperature. If the individuals in a particular room complain of excessive heat or cooling, the immediate solution would be to shut the vent on the grille or use furniture to block the airflow. This is not a permanent solution since it doesn't address the reasons why the room has inadequate or excessive airflow. Additionally, blocking the airflow such as adding partitions can cause parts of the room to be much colder or hotter than the rest.

Boilers

Following building codes, a boiler must be properly inspected and maintained to ensure that no leaks occur that could release harmful carbon monoxide into the building or cause an explosion. Additionally, the boiler system must operate efficiently so it does not expend wasted energy. Standards exist to determine how much combustion air is needed in order to burn the fuel used to heat the home or building. Items to consider regarding boiler operation are whether the boiler produces high enough temperatures to heat a building. Also, whether the boiler receives enough combustion air to perform well. Inspection and maintenance of gaskets is an important step to ensure that the boiler does not release carbon monoxide into the facility. Finally, the fuel lines should be inspected also so that gas fumes does not permeate the building causing illness to the occupants

Air Filter Selection

Air filters must be periodically inspected and cleaned or replaced to ensure that proper airflow is maintained and that the indoor air quality has not been compromised. Lower efficiency air filters are the least expensive to purchase, however, the structure of the filter itself has a tendency to become deformed as it fills up with the dust and particles which it has entrapped. When the filtration is no longer sufficient, airflow through that particular airway becomes sluggish and requires more energy to pass through. Most facilities and HVAC system designers recommend a medium efficiency air filter since the pleated design allows for better filtration and also it does not have to be replaced as often. An unchecked filter can reduce the air quality of the system and can lead to microbacterial growth if condensation is allowed to flourish on the filter. Most often, the filters that are the easiest to access by use of a latch or hinged door, versus a bolted panel, are the ones that are replaced most often, leading to cleaner air in that portion of the facility.

Air Filtration Rating

Air filters are designed to prevent the passage of contaminants into the HVAC system that would then cause health problems and clog the ductwork. Lack of proper filtration can decrease the efficiency of the system and cause it to use more energy to heat and cool the air. A filter is generally tested in terms of dust spots and arrestance, which is a measure of how well it captures synthetic particles. A low efficiency air filter is generally used to eliminate common dust and lint from plugging heating and cooling coils. It is rated by the ASHRAE standard in the range of 10-20% efficiency. Medium efficiency air filters are rated in the 30-60% range and can provide better filtration. These filters use accordion style surfaces to get the maximum amount of contaminants such as bacteria, mold, fungus, pollen, and dirt. Finally, a high efficiency air filter can clear up to 90% of the contaminants in the air. The rating to seek out for a particular HVAC unit depends on the amount of energy needed to ensure that airflow continues to flow through the system, yet still be able to pass through filtration.

Thermostat Controls

HVAC units can be controlled by manual or automatic controls, although usually a combination of both is needed. These controls can turn on the unit, turn it off, regulate the temperature, open and shut the dampers, and control the fan speed. The larger the facility, the more complex and automated the system becomes. Home systems tend to be simpler in nature; however, the control and temperature systems need to have a back up battery system in place in the event of power outages. With this backup, the system can reset itself. The area in which thermostat controls can generally be found is inside of a room. If the controls are set in direct sunlight or close to equipment that gives off heat such as a copy machine, then the temperature in the room will be not be at a comfortable level for the occupants.

Humidity Controls

Air leaks in the duct system can cause the unit to work less efficiently, using more energy to heat or cool a room than necessary. It can decrease the life expectancy of the ductwork and reduce the indoor air quality immensely. The filtration system will be rendered useless as contaminants may not pass through proper filtration but leak out from the sides of the ductwork into the rooms. If the leakage point is underneath the facility such as in a crawl space, contamination from soils and mold may ensue. Leakage can also occur at joints, seams, and connectors in the ductwork. Testing for leakage is part of the inspection that must be performed on a regular basis. The return plenum is yet another source of leakage if the control thermostats are not operating properly and much of the air being generated in the plenum is wasted by not releasing it back into the rooms.

Contaminant Growth

The design of the HVAC system requires that the airflow traveling over coils allows the air to either heat or cool to the degree to which the building occupants will feel most comfortable. If these coils were to malfunction, then adverse temperature changes would occur. If there are leaks in the coils or in the overall system, condensation may occur causing bacteria, molds, and fungus to develop. During the cooling process, condensation develops which is then collected in a drain pan underneath the coils. The condensation is then expelled through a trap. If there is an insufficient seal, water may back up and then bacteria may develop in the standing water. During the heating process, a similar situation can occur in which the hot water inside the heating coil may be set at too low of a temperature causing the system to not condition the outside air properly.

Leakage

A supply fan is one design element that has the potential for change. As the building is constructed, space must be shared with other parts of construction such as electrical supplies, framework, etc. and thus, the size of the fan can vary depending on the route the ductwork will take. To effectively deliver the air throughout the facility, it is important to match the size of the supply fan to the length of duct that the airflow is expected to travel. The performance of the fan is rated as "cfm", which stands for cubic feet per minute, at a set airflow resistance. The size of the ductwork and the velocity of the air traveling within it determine the airflow. The path that the ductwork takes also plays a role in how quickly the air travels throughout the system, allowing for directional changes. The supply fan, therefore, must correspond with the distance of the ductwork, velocity of the airflow, and also the size of the ductwork in order to function properly. If these criteria are not met, the airflow will be substandard.

Ductwork Replacement

When the system has been found contain damage such as from water or tears in the ductwork, it is necessary to replace that section to ensure that the air quality is not further compromised. If the interior lining of ductwork has water damage, that is a potential breeding ground for bacteria and mold which can then be distributed back into the facility. Prior to replacing the damaged ductwork, it is important to identify the cause of the initial damage and repair that problem quickly. To simply replace the ductwork without correcting the issue will only cause further problems down the road. During the inspection process, more consideration should be paid to ductwork that has a greater surface area over which the air travels. Fibrous glass ductwork can trap more contaminants than sheet metal, so greater care must be taken when cleaning these types of ducts to refrain from loosening these fibers.

Dirt

All homes and businesses generate dust and dirt from day to day activities. As such, minimal amounts are considered normal in the HVAC unit. Dust and dirt can affect many components of the HVAC system from coils, ductwork, to the housing and can redistribute this dust back into the air. When the dust and dirt is excessive, problems arise in which the buildup of dust in the ductwork causes the unit to run less efficiently, using more power to provide the same amount of cooling or heating as before, and can contribute to a host of health problems that arise from breathing contaminated air. In order to reduce the potential for this problem becoming more serious, regular cleaning of the home or facility is necessary to remove excessive dust. Additionally, cleaning of the drain pans, inspecting for leaks in the system, and making any necessary repairs due to water damage will ensure that further contamination does not occur.

Air Duct Cleaning

It is important that the location where duct cleaning is to be performed is free of all necessary personnel to limit their exposure to chemicals, debris and particles. While cleaning, it is important that all the exhaust created by the cleaning is transmitted outside and away from areas where people are located. If access doors are created to clean the interior of the duct, the priority should be to use doors that are already cut into the ductwork. It is important to maintain as closely as possible the original integrity of the ducting. When vacuums are use to remove particulate matter, the changes are greater that the negative pressure will cause the ducting to collapse. Also, gentle cleanings are necessitated for those ducts made out of fibrous glass as these have a tendency to send up small particles of the lining into the air. As a measure of further precaution, HEPA filtration is necessary in areas where vacuum collection takes place within an occupied space.

Cooling Tower and a Water Chiller Guidelines

It is important to periodically clean and maintain a cooling tower in order to prevent the growth of micro bacteria and other biological particles that may contaminate the water used to cool the building. Additionally, sediment and other debris may lodge near the bottom of the tower and these must be removed also. It is important to wear protective equipment to prevent contamination from this debris. A water chiller needs to operate at lease 45 degrees or colder for maximum removal of moisture in the air during times of humidity. A possibility for hazards exists when the water leaks out of the chiller causing chemicals to spill out. It is important to ensure that any leaks are repaired quickly and that any wastes from the refrigerant be disposed of in a proper manner.

Microbial Particle Prevention

A regular cycle of cleaning and maintenance goes a long way in prevention. After cleaning the surfaces of the ductwork, coils, and other components, it is imperative to completely rinse and dry these chemicals away so that they cannot be blown through the system and out into occupant areas, posing a health risk. When components have been damaged by water or condensation, it is important to completely replace these components so that further damage will be prevented. Even if the perception is that these areas are thoroughly cleaned, small particles not visible to the naked eye may still be present and harbor additional bacterial growth. A regular inspection, repair, and maintenance schedule will ensure that the filters, dampers, coils, condensers, and exhaust fans are operating at full potential, thus increasing the life of the HVAC system as a whole.

Contamination Substance Evaluation

When considering a substance that will protect against future contamination of bacteria, microbial particles, mold, and fungus, it is important to get one that has been rated by the EPA to perform that specific job. Most biocides, as they are known, are sanitizers, and not chemicals that are designed to disinfect or sterilize the surfaces of the ductwork. Their role is to prevent the growth of these types of particles. Sealants generally are not recommended to stop growth of micro-bacterial particles since their application can affect the surface of the ducting and the degree to which the air flows through it and can deteriorate the interior lining. Additionally, the sealant could cause harmful effects on the occupants of the building as well as create a potential for fire hazards.

ASHRAE Standards

Information contained within the ASHRAE standard for "Thermal Environmental Conditions for Human Occupancy" covers a wide variety of conditions such as temperature, humidity, and air movement. It details the type of indoor air conditions needed for occupant comfort in both summer and winter conditions. It also presents different scenarios depending on the activity level of the occupants in the facility, whether they are more physically active such as in a gym, or sedentary, such as in an office environment. Conditions for creating optimum humidity levels are explained in this standard and limitations on the range of temperature readings in a given space are listed. Finally, guidelines are listed for ensuring occupant comfort as it relates to temperature, relative humidity, air movement, and floor temperatures.

The ASHRAE standard for "Ventilation for Acceptable Air Quality" was developed to help with the design process of ensuring that ventilation and air quality is met when building a new facility. Divided into two parts, this standard goes into great detail on the design of ventilation systems and the protocol to ensure air quality. Under the section covering ventilation rate, the extent of air quality is determined by the size of the space, number of occupants, and the amount of outdoor air within that given space. Tables are listed within this standard for easy calculations and reference. The air quality procedure cites that controlling and restricting the amount of known contaminants within the air can achieve the proper air quality. The information garnered as a result of following the standard must be made permanently available to the owner of the building once the HVAC system has been installed. Other parts to this standard include defining ventilation, providing recommendations for exhaust and heat recovery, and listing guidelines for the control of contaminants.

The ASHRAE guideline for the "Commissioning for HVAC Systems" describes the documentation necessary to show that a particular HVAC unit has met the requirements as set in the design of the system. In this documentation, it must be noted as to the original intent of the HVAC system in the number of occupants the system is designed to support as well as the square footage and building size it can control in temperature. This standard also describes the method used for testing the system and ways to make adjustments that allow for deviances in occupancy rates and also building additions as they arise. It also allows for training procedures for the main operator of the HVAC system and also maintenance schedules and commissioning.

The ASHRAE standard for "Method of Testing Air-Cleaning Devices Used in General Ventilation for Removing Particulate Matter" explains the degree to which one can evaluate the effectiveness of air cleaning devices and vacuum systems in how well they remove contaminants from the air. The methodology used to determine this is calculated in two different processes. The first is the weight arrestance test that measures the amounts of large and heavy particles of dust and debris that are trapped by a low efficiency filter. To conduct this test, synthetic particles are sent through a filter and then the measure is taken to determine the result. These can be compared to the next test, which is the atmospheric dust spot test. This second test determines the efficiency of both the air cleaner system and medium efficiency air cleaners. In conducting this test, the removal rate is determined by how well the filters prevent an area from becoming soiled as particulate matter is forced against it. The ratings on these two tests are not interchangeable and one cannot do a direct comparison based on the results.

AIR FILTERING TERMS

Air Filtration Device: A device composed of a blower assembly, which pushes air through a filtration system before releasing the air back into the room or space.

Air Scrubber: A type of air filtration device that uses re-circulated air that has been put through HEPA (high efficiency particulate absorption) filtration. HEPA filtration must have an efficiency rating of 99.97% at 0.3 micron sized particles.

Air Handling Unit: A device which is self-contained that filters, conditions, and cleans the air prior to being exhausted through the space. These AHUs are connected to ductwork as the mode of transportation of the conditioned air.

ACR 2005 STANDARD

The ACR 2005 is designed to provide guidelines relating to the industry standards when it comes to HVAC inspection, cleaning, remediation, and performance assessments. The design of the HVAC system from its beginnings in a manufacturing shop to the installation process show how dust and particulate matter is an ongoing problem to overcome. The ACR 2005 also provides a recommended schedule for system inspection to help determine whether remediation is warranted. It also outlines which components of the system need to be evaluated on a regular basis. Also, this standard identifies the common forms of contaminants that one can expect to find in and on the HVAC coils, condensers, drip pans, and ductwork. Finally, the topic of environmental engineering controls is addressed to inform the contractors of the need for protective measures on behalf of the building's occupants to protect them from any cross contamination during the remediation process.

ACRONYMS

Acronym	Meaning
ASHRAE	American Society of Heating, Refrigerating, and Air-Conditioning Engineers
ASCS	Air Systems Cleaning Specialist
ACGIH	American Conference of Governmental Industrial Hygienists
AIHA	American Industrial Hygiene Association
ASTM	American Society for Testing and Materials
IAQA	Indoor Air Quality Association
EPA	Environmental Protection Agency
IKECA	International Kitchen Exhaust Cleaning Association
NAIMA	North American Insulation Manufacturers Association
NFPA	National Fire Protection Association
OSHA	Occupational Safety and Health Administration
SMACNA	Sheet Metal and Air-Conditioning Contractors' National Association

AIR HANDLING UNITS

Central Station Air Handling Unit: A device with the capacity to perform cleaning, heating, cooling, circulating, humidifying, and dehumidifying the air.

Cooling/Heating Unit: Performs heating and cooling functions.

Cooling Unit: Performs cooling functions only.

Heating Unit: Performs heating functions only.

Make-up Air Unit: Primary role is to replace the volume of air that has been exhausted.

Ventilating Unit: Primary role is to provide ventilation only.

Mold Inspection

Most facilities, whether residential or industrial, are on an inspection schedule of anywhere from one to two years. While performing the inspection of the air handling unit and supply and return ducts, it can be noted whether there is the presence of mold and of it is rated as conditions 1, 2, or 3. HVAC systems located in a hot or humid climate need to be inspected more often due to the greater potential for developing mold and fungal growth. If the preliminary inspection includes trace amounts of mold, the services of an IEP may be contracted to determine the extent of the contamination as well as the procedure for eliminating the mold and finding a solution to prevent further growth. If the mold growth is in an isolated area and is easily removed, then the services of an IEP generally are not required. If there are extensive amounts of mold growth, then it is recommended to seek out any potential leakage leading to water damage that may have contributed to the growth.

As an example: A remediation contractor has determined that there is mold infestation within the system and an indoor environmental professional confirmed this. The next steps, prior to initiating the cleaning, include the following information.

When diagnosing mold infestation in a facility, the cleaning work should not progress until a project evaluation has been completed and a plan of action is determined. Including in the evaluation are three steps to follow: determining the usage of the building, identifying the specific type of contamination that was found in that facility, and conducting a survey on the environmental impact that cleaning would have on the indoor air. Using visual inspections of the structure of the system, the contractors would determine the structural integrity of the system and its components. The evaluation can determine the details of the project to include the types of repair work to be made to the system, the techniques used for cleaning the condition 2 or 3 mold or fungus, and also account for any environmental engineering controls that would protect the building's occupants.

During the inspection process, if any of the following conditions are found, then it is necessary to perform a thorough cleaning of the system: When the system is no longer producing the correct volume of air, the air flow drops, and the unit appears to expend more energy to either heat or cool, then a cleaning may be necessary to rid the system of built up contaminants. At times, dust and debris may be seen blowing through grilles into the spaces or it may be visually seen during the inspection process. If patches of mold growth can be seen in the inspection and it is confirmed by an IEP that condition 2 or 3 is present, then a thorough cleaning should take place. Finally, if the air-handling unit appears to be adversely affecting the health of the occupants, then measures should be taken, including cleaning, that would improve the indoor air quality.

Credentials

In order to successfully perform HVAC remediation, a person needs to have extensive training in the mechanisms that comprise an HVAC system. Knowledge of the components, their function, their capabilities, and the design of the system as a whole are needed to fully be aware of the processes by which these components work with one another. Techniques in inspection, cleaning, and restoration are expected to be performed according to industry standards and practices. Certifications are an added degree of security as the person is shown to have undergone extensive practice and knowledge to be awarded their certification. Finally, in order to determine conditions 1, 2, or 3, the person must also be knowledgeable in mold bacterial identification and elimination as well as environmental engineering controls.

Conditions 1, 2, and 3

In reference to the levels of mold growth in an HVAC system, the ranking follows either Condition 1, 2, or 3. A person with experience in reading the ecology of the mold spores can determine the rating and also make recommendations on return the system to its proper level. Condition 1 refers to a normal ecological system with expected levels of fungal spores and growth that would be considered common in an indoor environment. Condition 2 refers to having an amount of settled spores and traces of growth that appear to have come from an area noted as Condition 3. This last condition is the environment where actual mold and fungal growth has occurred and is either active or dormant. Using research, data collection, and analysis, the indoor environmental professional can outline a plan of action to remove the cause of the fungal growth and can design a plan to return the environment to Condition 1.

Engineering Assessments

It is recommended that an engineering assessment be performed on a periodic basis to ensure that the system is working in the intent by which it was designed. Relying on the design specifications along with any modifications that were made to the system, the engineers can determine if the unit is working as efficiently as it was intended based upon the numbers of occupants as well as the square footage of the facility it is designed to handle. If the temperature and the relative humidity cannot be maintained according to ASHRAE standards or if the temperature varies within a region and it not fixed through remediation, then an assessment must be performed to determine where the system efficiency has broken down. Potentially, it may be determined that the system is suffering some form of mechanical failure or that which may be a result of age of the unit and its lack of capacity for meeting demand.

Occasionally, engineering assessments determine that the HVAC unit was not designed or commissioned properly.

Building Terms

Residential: Consists of apartments, single-family homes, and condominiums.

Industrial: Manufacturing facilities, material processing centers, or storage of products.

Commercial: Facilities utilizing HVAC systems greater than ten tons or 4000cfm airflow.

Light Commercial: Facilities utilizing HVAC systems of up to ten tons or 4000 cfm airflow.

Restaurant: The seating area and workspaces are classified as commercial use; however, the kitchen area falls under another standard.

Healthcare: Hospitals, nursing homes, outpatient facilities, or any other building whose use is to care for those with compromised immune systems.

Marine: Any ship or floating vessel.

Special Use: Areas that need to maintain strict environmental controls in terms of lighting, climate, and cleanliness. This includes laboratories or clean rooms.

Multi-Use: Facilities where more than one building use can be found under one roof. In this scenario, the use that requires stricter controls takes precedence.

Building Usage

Building use classification is simply a definition of the capacity of the building and the primary function it serves for its occupants. Because cleaning techniques can vary depending on building use, it is important to identify which classification a structure falls under. Broken down into many categories, building usage can be either industrial, residential, marine, commercial, light commercial, restaurant, healthcare, special use or multi-use facilities. The level to which the project scope can vary depends on the use of the building, as does the types of cleaning procedures to follow and the level of cleanliness one must adhere to. One aspect of the indoor environmental professional is to assist with determining the category of building usage a structure falls under and then develop a coordinated plan of action appropriate for that facility.

Pressurization

In order to prevent particulate matter from spreading out to other occupied areas, it is important to maintain the right pressure differential relative to the surrounding spaces in which occupants may reside. This can be accomplished through the use of a negative air machine or equipment that has been outfitted with HEPA filtration. Pressurization is important regardless of the classification of the building's use.

This pressurization only applies to the portion of the building currently being worked on, not the entire system. Parts of the system that are being worked on must be closed off to prevent cross contamination and to maintain the right pressure differential.

Environment Engineering Controls

Environmental engineering controls are designed to protect the occupants of a facility from further contamination either through improperly removing the contaminants from the ventilation system or through not protecting the facility during the cleaning process. Using instruments such as manometers, laser particle counters, or other measuring devices, the IEP can detect whether the environmental controls are working properly. Prior to performing the cleaning, an indoor environmental impact survey must be completed which will determine the process in which to avoid contaminating other areas of the facility and lessen the risk to workers and to building occupants. Examples of environments engineering controls would involve putting up barriers to contain dust, fumes, and other particles within the area being cleaned, using HEPA filtration on vacuum systems, and also methods for suppressing dust accumulation while cleaning.

Safety Concerns

In cases where it is necessary to disable the safety measures such as detection systems for smoke and fire, the appropriate authorities must be notified. Modifications may be made that would temporarily deactivate the system and prevent detection of smoke or fire in the HVAC system and the building itself. Special building permits may be necessary. A back up plan must be instigated and evacuation plans should be developed that will ensure the safety of the building's occupants during the cleaning. After the cleaning process has been completed, the safety devices should be tested, confirmed, and documented that they are working properly before the job can be considered complete. The responsibility for ensuring that the correct procedures are being followed rests with the building owner and his or her manager.

Equipment Decontamination

There is the potential for introducing contaminants into a new area if cleaning equipment such as tools, vacuum systems, and other instruments used in remediation have not been thoroughly cleaned prior to performing a cleaning job. The responsibility in maintaining the integrity of the tools rests with the HVAC remediation company. The building owner or the worksite manager should be the person to review and inspect the equipment prior to it being brought into his facility if the equipment has been used to restore a condition 3 area back to condition 1. In order to completely remove any contaminants, tools and equipment it must be inspected, serviced, cleaned, washed, and dried before putting them into storage. This procedure applies to all areas regardless of the classification of the building's usage.

Equipment Redundancy

On the facility worksite, considering the high degree of contaminants that must be contained, there exists the potential for equipment breakdown. To counter this, the recommendation is for additional pieces of equipment to be present onsite that will perform the same duties of the job and meet or exceed the safety and performance requirements of the remediation. Oftentimes, equipment redundancy is stated in the project outline provided at the onset of the cleaning while in the planning stages. Redundant equipment is rated for concurrent or non-concurrent use. Concurrent means that the equipment is used in the same containment area for the same cleaning project. It must meet or exceed the same standards as the primary equipment before being brought into the containment area. Non-concurrent use indicates that type of equipment that is present on the job site, but not actively in use to perform the cleaning unless there is a malfunction of the primary equipment.

Remediation Project Outline

The areas that need to be covered in presenting an outline for the scope of the remediation project include:

- A monitoring plan for ensuring the project is completed.
- A detailed outline of the work to be completed.
- The groups of trades that will be involved in different aspects of the cleaning process.
- The number of people working on the project.
- The number of man-hours until completion (estimate).
- The calendar schedule of the project step by step until completion.
- The cleaning methods to be utilized as well as the equipment to be used.
- Safety plans and evacuation plans.
- SDS data sheets.
- Documentation to be provided to the building's owner to use for a future baseline.

Contaminated Waste Removal

In order to prevent cross contamination of hazardous materials, it is required that disposal of the debris should be made in double sealed polyethylene bags that are greater than 6ml thick. These bags must be sealed prior to removing them from the containment area and should be compliant with all laws and codes relating to the disposal of hazardous waste materials. After removing the bags from the facility, they must be placed into a secure truck or container away from the possibility of anyone tampering with them. In the event of a bag tearing outside the facility, then cordoning off the space and vacuuming the area using HEPA filtration is necessary to control the spread of the debris. Any vacuum devices that were used in the remediation process should also be double bagged and secured prior to removing them from the site. If servicing is required, it must be done on site and in a negatively pressurized area. Any ductwork and debris that does not contain asbestos or lead by products may be put into normal disposal containers; however, these bags should also be securely contained.

Cleaning Outline

Included in the inspection and cleaning process of the HVAC system are all the components, ductwork, grilles, supply fans, exhaust, condensate drainage pans, heating and cooling coils, etc. that make up the assembly which drives conditioned air throughout the facility. These devices can be cleaned in any number of ways specific to the type of material each component is constructed of. Mechanical cleaning devices such as vacuums, agitation systems, brushes, pressurized water, etc. are used in areas where more forceful removal methods will not damage the component. A collection device is generally used to capture the debris that is dislodged from the components during the cleaning process. Vacuum collection devices sometimes require HEPA filtration depending on the particulate matter being removed. Finally, power washing, steam cleaning, or wet cleaning is used in areas where the component will not be damaged by the liquid itself and by the pressure from the liquid.

Condition 2 or Condition 3 Processes

Special care must be taken when cleaning these types of environments due to the concern over recontamination of other areas of the facility. When areas are found to contain high levels or mold, fungus, or spores, these areas need to be cordoned off and the removal of these components must be performed prior to a complete HVAC system remediation. In the event that this is not possible, then steps must be taken to ensure that once a section of the HVAC system is cleaned, it is protected from further contamination by those parts of the system that are not yet cleaned. Supplemental heating and cooling may need to be brought in to provide for the comfort of building occupants. When the contaminated areas are rebuilt or repaired, construction debris may infiltrate the system and areas cleaned prior may then need to be recleaned before the HVAC system remediation can be considered complete.

Important Terms

Mechanical agitation: The practice of utilizing cleaning techniques such as power brushes, contact vacuuming, electric brushes, cable driven brushes, etc. to remove debris from inside a chamber then towards a vacuum device for collection.

Contact vacuuming: The use of a vacuum system with a brush attachment to remove dust and debris from the system. Generally utilizes HEPA filtration in this procedure.

Component cleaning: The cleaning of all parts of the HVAC system according to standards.

Wet cleaning: Utilizing power brushes, sprayers, and steam cleaning to clean all components of an HVAC that are not adversely affected by liquids. Any chemicals used during the cleaning process must comply with all national and state regulation and be applied according to manufacturers instructions.

Velocity Levels

Contaminants vary in size from a light sprinkling of fine dust particles to up to heavy dusts. For particles at the lighter end of the scale such as cotton lint, wood flour, or litho powder, a velocity range of 2500-3000 fpm will suffice to remove these contaminants from the system. The next larger size contaminant is known as dry dusts and powders that take 3000-4000 fpm to remove them. Examples of these types include powder dust, soap dust, and shavings. Average industrial dust is generally found as powder from grinding, clay dust, buffing dust, and limestone dust and needs 3500- 4000 fpm to remove it from the system. Heavy dusts consisting of sawdust, metal shavings, sandblasting dust, and lead shavings, needs 4000-4500 fpm to successfully remove it from the system.

Condenser Coil Cleaning

It must be determined whether the coils can be cleaned while remaining in place or by removing them entirely in order to avoid contamination by the wet cleaning process. The purpose of the cleaning process is to get the coils to a visibly clean state. Use of cleaning chemicals should be done in accordance with manufacturer's instructions and also according to standards. Additionally, the chemicals must be tested to ensure that irreparable damage is not done to the coils. Some chemicals are considered no-rinse, but to be on the safe side a thorough clean water rinse may be necessary to completely remove all traces of the chemical. For heavily contaminated coils, it is recommended that they be removed from the system during cleaning. If this is not possible, then other nearby components in the air-handling unit need to be protected from damage by the wet cleaning process. If they are, then these components will need to be replaced prior to completing the job.

Wet Cleaning

In order to thoroughly clean the air handling unit, it is important that measures be taken to ensure that a drainage device be tested and in place prior to beginning the job. Additionally, any materials present, such as fiberglass insulation should not become wet otherwise the product loses its insulating abilities. To best clean the components of the air-handling unit, mechanical scrubbing methods are utilized. All interior components such as condensers, coils, blowers, etc. are to be cleaned thoroughly. During cleanings to remove accumulated mold, components may need to be cleaned several times over to ensure the cleanest possible surface and to inhibit further growth. All areas that are cleaned must comply with standards particular to that material or component.

Mold Contamination Concerns

Any mold-contaminated component must be aggressively cleaned or else the affected parts should be removed and disposed of. Any porous surfaces that have been contaminated by mold, as in Condition 3, should be completely replaced. Using care in removing these parts to prevent further contamination, they must first be properly disposed of. Following that step, it is important to use mechanical agitation such as brushes and vacuum systems to clean the non-porous surface areas underneath the fiber insulation, for example. After ensuring that there are not any additional areas of mold contamination, then the contractor may replace the discarded surfaces in the system. These non-porous surfaces must be cleaned until they can pass the cleanliness verification standards.

Other Coil Types

When cleaning electric coils, all power to the system must be disconnected and the system shut down according to OSHA standards and lockout/tagout. If the wet cleaning process is utilized to clean the coils, then a non-corrosive detergent cleaner must be used and the coils thoroughly rinsed and dried prior to reactivating the system. In cleaning hydronic coils, the biggest challenge arises in trying to capture the cleaning water in a system that does not have a drain pan underneath to capture the spent water and cleaning chemicals. Generally, when there is no visible collection of mold growth present on the exterior of the coils, a simple cleaning through mechanical means is sufficient, however, if an IEP has determined through testing that the level is at a Condition 2 or higher, than wet cleaning of the coils is required.

Fiberglass Duct Liners and Boards

The best procedure by which to clean fiberglass duct liners and boards should be done using HEPA filtration due to the small size of the particles that make up the liners. Also important in cleaning is to have negative pressure in the immediate vicinity while cleaning this component. In the event that moisture seeps into the liner or the fiberboards, they must be evaluated and possibly completely replaced as their integrity may then have been compromised. Any mechanical cleaning that is to be performed should not cause any tears, breaks, or rips in the fiber lining. The cleaning must be done to comply with and pass the cleanliness verification regulations. Thermal acoustic fiberglass liners must be replaced if any tears or abrasions are found in them and if they are unable to be repaired using a standard treatment or coating products applied after the cleaning has been performed.

Surface Treatments

Surface treatments are used to restore the integrity of a component as a temporary measure until actual cleaning and remediation is performed. These treatments are best performed on porous surfaces that have been cleaned and verified as to cleanliness according to standards. They can also be used to make minor repairs in the surface of the components. Surface treatments can also consist of an antimicrobial coating that is designed to further provide a protective layer to inhibit mold growth. These chemicals must also be applied according to the manufacturer's guidelines and also in accordance with the Environmental Protection Agency. They must also be designated as safe for use in HVAC systems and their use must have been deemed necessary for that particular system.

Replacing Thermal Acoustic Liners

Once the old liner has been removed, the surface needs to be scraped clean and all visible dust and debris removed. If the contamination was the result of mold, then the duct needs to be returned to Condition 1 status prior to the installation of the new lining. The installation of this lining must be compliant with SMACNA and NAIMA standards. Additionally, the materials used must meet or exceed any state or national codes for that HVAC system. All the joints must be properly sealed with mastic or metal nosing to comply with industry standards. After all the new materials have been installed, it is important that the new lining meet the verification cleanliness standards. Occasionally, the new lining must be cleaned after installation in order to meet these verification cleanliness standards.

RESURFACING FIBERGLASS

Resurfacing of the duct liner or board is necessary when it appears that the surface has become compromised either through excessive tears, abrasions, or during normal use. Resurfacing also is performed when the surface of the fiberboards needs to be replaced to comply with a more efficient design, such as one with a surface that attracts more particulate matter. It must be assessed prior to cleaning whether or not the new surface is capable of bonding to the surface of the component. If the material is not deemed suitable, then it must be completely replaced. If the material is bondable then resurfacing may not be necessary. The material used in the resurfacing must have a fire rating that complies with local codes and also be applied in accordance with manufacturer's instructions and must pass the cleanliness verification.

HVAC SYSTEM DAMAGE

During a flood or excessive water situation, water can enter the system and, depending on how long before the water dries out, can cause the growth of fungus, bacteria, and mold. The system components must be evaluated to see the extent of the damage and whether or not these components can be restored to their original condition or must be replaced. The cleaning standards, environmental engineering controls, and methodologies are determined by the IICRC standards and are based on the category of water that caused the damage. Fire and smoke damage also needs to be evaluated during the cleaning process and any components that cannot be cleaned according to standards must be replaced. Additionally, porous surfaces must be evaluated because the smoke damage and resulting debris could be blown through the ductwork to other parts of the facility. Odors may have been absorbed and could still be present in the insulation.

RESTORATION AND REPAIR CONDITIONS

In the event of damage to the ductwork, an evaluation must take place to assess the damage. In instances where the extent of the damage is not prevalent throughout the system, then sections of the system may undergo complete restoration or repair. Several causes that contribute to damage include fire, smoke, water, or flood damage. In the evaluation, the assessment of the extent of the damage is performed and then documented. This evaluation takes place during the cleaning process where a listing of all the components is detailed and a determination is made regarding which parts need to be repaired or replaced to preserve the integrity of the HVAC system. Any components of the HVAC system that are not able to withstand the methods of cleaning are considered damaged and should be replaced.

Project Management Plans

A project management plan should include the following procedures:

Meeting held at the outset of the project in which the project is discussed among the contractors.

- Documentation of the equipment to be used during the project.
- Verification of the conditions of the environment prior to the cleaning and bringing the equipment into the facility.
- Monitoring of the air quality during the remediation on behalf of the occupants.
- Ensuring chemicals and materials used during the cleaning process have been approved on site prior to use.
- Ensuring personal safety equipment is used while on site in the proper manner.
- Documenting all the areas that have been cleaned.
- Ensuring service openings are properly closed.
- Providing final documentation upon completion of the remediation process.

Project Monitoring Plan

The building owner or manager should be involved in every step of the remediation process. Included in this is their involvement in the cleaning process where the following issues must be addressed:

- Protecting the building occupants and employees during the remediation process.
- Containing the cleaning process in one area and protecting sensitive equipment.
- Protecting and deactivating the fire and smoke detectors in order to prevent false alarms.

Cleanliness Verification Methods

The system cleanliness verification is a series of tests to determine the cleanliness level of the system in relation to the standards. The test is divided into several parts: visual tests, surface comparison tests, and vacuum tests. The cleanliness verification is performed after cleaning and before the HVAC system is returned to use. Additionally, it is performed prior to any type of surface or antibacterial surface treatments have been applied. The cleanliness verification applies to all types of components including porous and non-porous surfaces. This test is not specific to determine the level of bacterial contamination, but to determine the cleanliness level after remediation has been performed. Also, the test does not indicate whether an HVAC system needs to be cleaned.

There are different methods employed to verify cleanliness:

- Method 1: Visual Inspection - Performed on both porous and non-porous surfaces to determine if there is any dust or debris on the components that make up the HVAC system. If cleanliness cannot be determined by this test, then the second test method should be performed.
- Method 2: Surface Comparison Test – Also used to test cleanliness of both metal and fiberglass surfaces. This test is conducted by testing the surface cleanliness both before and after a specific type of vacuum test is performed. This test uses a HEPA filtered contact vacuum with a brush attachment that is brushed over a specific area four times and then a visual test is conducted to determine any noticeable changes. If there are no changes, then the surface is considered cleaned. If the test is inconclusive, then the third method is utilized.
- Method 3: NADCA Vacuum test – This test evaluates any remaining particulate matter on the surface of the components. A template is placed over the surface of the component. A filtered cassette is laid over the template without touching it, and air is then forced over the template. After the test, the filtered cassette is weighed to determine the amount of particulate matter it was able to pick up.

NADCA Vacuum Test

The vacuum test involves the use of an air pump, filter media, a calibration device, and a template to determine whether the surface component passes the cleanliness verification test. The template is placed over the surface component and secured. The air-handling unit should be off during these preparations. The filtered cassette is then attached to the air pump tubing and calibrated to 15 liters per minute. The cassette is moved twice over the surface of the template and then weighed to determine the extent of the debris it picked up. An acceptable level is less than .75 milligrams per 100 square centimeters. This test can be conducted by an IEP and while some samples can be tested onsite, the filter cartridge is generally sealed and sent off to a laboratory for analysis.

Containment Engineering Strategies

Containment engineering strategies are designed to protect the building occupants during the remediation process. These strategies are customized according to the degree to which contamination has taken place in the facility. Level one containment requires minimum engineering controls. This applies to marine, residential, light commercial, and industrial, and requires that no mold or bacterial contamination be present. Level two containment can apply to any building classification. This level of containment is applied to those scenarios in which there is the presentation of mold and bacterial contamination. A decontamination unit is not necessary for this containment. Level three containment applies to facilities where there are high levels of micro bacterial contamination. This level requires a single chamber decontamination unit. Level four contamination uses a two-chamber decontamination unit. This applies to health care facilities or where there are hazardous levels of biological contaminants.

Level one containment engineering strategies apply to any residential, light commercial, industrial, or marine facilities. This level is designated if there is no known mold or bacterial contamination within the unit. To adhere to the guidelines for containment, a clean protective covering must be put in place in each work area to protecting the floor, computer equipment, and work areas of the occupants. If possible, this covering should be extended slightly outside the work area to ensure adequate protection and coverage. All equipment to be used in the remediation should be properly sealed and cleaned prior to bringing it into the facility. Inlet openings on the vacuum systems need to be sealed during transport. Any tools that travel through occupied spaces must be wet wiped and vacuumed with HEPA filtration prior to using them in the HVAC system. Finally, proper precautions must be taken to avoid cross contamination into occupied spaces.

Level two containment engineering strategies apply to those facilities in which the microbial contamination covers an area of less than five square feet. This level is the minimum containment level required for a healthcare facility. All the precautions followed under level one containment must be in addition to the guidelines under level two. This area must be negatively pressurized at all times. Any work performed above the ceiling must have a protective barrier on all sides of the occupied space using 6ml fire retardant polyethylene sheeting. The sheeting must be airtight on all sides and securely attached to the ceiling, walls, and floor. Additionally, the floor must be covered with a similar 6ml polyethylene sheet. A vertical entrance opening into this area is to be made no less than six inches from the floor and extending five feet up. Ensure that there is a double-sided flap to prevent particulate matter from entering this area. Before dismantling the containment area, it should be vacuumed using HEPA filtration and surfaces wet-wiped.

Level three containment strategies apply to areas where there is a severe contamination of micro-bacterial particles. All containment strategies of level one and two need to be followed. Level three containment is the level at which most healthcare facilities are remediated regardless if mold contamination exists. The area must be negatively pressurized to avoid the spread of airborne particles. A decontamination chamber must be attached to the containment area and secured in place. Monitoring of the background particulate matter must be conducted with a baseline measured prior to construction of the containment unit. Throughout the cleaning, measurements must be taken to ensure levels do not exceed the acceptable range and if they are found to be high, then the source of the leak must be found and corrected.

Level four containment includes all the precautions taken from levels one through three as well as additional precautions. Level four containment applies to healthcare facilities and those with hazardous levels of biological contaminants. This plan allows for the construction of a two-chamber decontamination unit which must be secured in place and not allow any particles to seep outside the containment area. In addition, a monitoring system set up to measure the amount of particles in the air both prior to and during the remediation should be utilized. Oftentimes, this system comes outfitted with an alarm designed to notify the contractors when the levels of particulate matter exceed an acceptable range.

Component Engineering Controls

HVAC component engineering controls refers to the ability to maintain the proper cleaning environment for each of the various components of the HVAC system and also in relation to the type of mold or bacterial contamination present. Common controls include maintaining negative pressurization to prevent the disbursement of airborne particles during the cleaning process, containment at a suitable level depending on the type of particles being cleaned from the components, and also on the measured area being cleaning. If the measured area of the component is less than 3 square meters, then the area must be cleaned accordingly with HEPA filtration vacuum systems or wet wiping. If the area is larger than 3 square meters and the component is located within an occupied space, then the containment must be processed according to level two guidelines. Severe levels of microbial contamination warrants cleaning a level two requirements or higher.

Laser Particle Counters

The laser particle counter must operate at a flow rate of 0.1 CFMs while performing the sampling. First, the counter must be checked to ensure that it has sufficient battery power to complete the sampling. Second, the date and time must be accurately programmed and the printer option must be set on. Once the counter is powered up, then the purge filter must be attached and run in concentration mode for one minute. At the end of the minute, print out a reading, remove the purge filter, and turn off the unit. Finally, replace the purge filter with the sampling probe. Three samples should be taken at the return air. The range values of the samples to be tested are 0.1, 0.3, 0.5, 0.7, 1.0, 2.0, and 5.0 micrometers. The laser particle counter must be calibrated at the factory prior to initial use and must be kept to a regular maintenance schedule to assure high performance.

Particle Profiles

This procedure is generally performed when the need for knowledge of the types of particulate matter and the location or origin is within the HVAC system must be made known. The point of capture is made prior to the location where the air is sent through the filtration process. The procedure for collecting the samples is usually performed by an IEP with the samples sent to a lab for analysis. In order to collect the sample, the IEP must first perform a visual inspection of the entire HVAC unit as a whole to include the interior, the by pass system, and the cabinet housing the main part of the unit. Documentation, both written and photo, should be made of the observations. Measurements of the particles taken at both the return and supply air registers are made with a laser particle counter. These are then plotted on a filter chart. Air samples are taken using a fungal spore trap, which will identify the type and amount of fungal spores, vitreous fibers, and other particles. A surface sampling is made using adhesive tape with these samples also sent to a lab for analysis. Finally, temperature and humidity readings are taken and measured against the requirements in the ASHRAE standards.

Air Samples

Air sampling is conducted to determine the amount of fungal spores that are present in the HVAC system. This procedure is performed using a fungal spore trap and the pump used to obtain the sample must be calibrated according to the cassette manufacturer's instructions. Three samples must be taken: one each of the return air, supply air, and the ambient indoor air. In order to take the samples a specific procedure must be followed. First, the spore trap should be attached to the pump and the inlet cover or seal removed. The sample pump should then be put into place for the designated period of time to allow for the collection of the sample. Supply air samples should be placed where they will not get air from ambient return air. Return air samples should be obtained in such a way as to not get outside air in the sample. Once all the samples have been obtained, they are analyzed in a laboratory and the results reported as spores per cubic meter.

The procedure in performing the sampling using the laser particle counter is as follows:

- Set the unit to indicate the number of samples you wish to obtain.
- Set the period to one minute.
- Set the print function on.
- Set the counter to a representative number for the project.
- Set the counter in the place where the sample needs to be taken and hold there for the designated time while counter is running.
- After sampling is completed, remove counter and replace with isokinetic probe.
- Set the number of samples the same as those taken in the return air.
- Set the counter to a representative number for the project.
- Now, sample the supply ducts by putting the isokinetic probe into the registers using a different one per sample.
- Continue this procedure until all samples have been collected.

Surface Samples

Applying an adhesive tape to the surface of a component, and then attaching the tape to a slide for analysis allows the contractor to obtain surface samples from the HVAC system. A series of five different samples need to be obtained from the following areas: the return duct, the air-handling unit, and the supply plenum or the supply duct. To perform the testing, the contractor or IEP must wear protective gloves while handling the tape or the slides. The adhesive tape should then be placed over the area to be tested. The tape, once lifted off, must then be placed onto the slide without touching any other object so as not to contaminate the sample. The slide is then sent off for analysis. Any spores or fungus found on the slides will be confirmed by the laboratory. The test will determine whether the HVAC system needs to be cleaned and to what extent the contamination has presented itself in the system.

Service Openings

Service openings in the HVAC system can generally be located in the following areas:

- Next to dampers, such as fire, control, or back draft.
- At duct transitions and changes of direction.
- Adjacent to heating and cooling coils.
- Next to other components and sensors.
- In close proximity to electric heat strips.
- Close to VAV boxes.

Service openings are located in these areas to allow for easy access to the interior for cleaning and inspection. When they are poorly constructed, it decreases the structural integrity of the system and can interfere with the fire safety rating.

Accident Preplanning

Proper planning is essential to ensure that all persons at a facility know the procedures to follow in the event of an accident. The accident planning should cover areas such as first aid, alarm systems, limiting the potential for harm to other personnel or equipment, and who to notify in the event of an accident. Also covered in the session should be the items needed in the accident investigation kit such as a camera, film, clipboard, graph paper, pens, and safety gear in the event that access into a damaged portion of the facility needs to be made. Safety gear can be comprised of items such as a hard hat, safety glasses, hearing protection, protective covering, and gloves. These items may be added to the accident investigation kit.

Accident Aftermath

An accident occurs due to lack of planning and not following proper safety procedures. The goals of an accident investigation are to determine the cause of an accident and identify the steps necessary to prevent the accident from recurring. The person in charge of the investigation will be performing an in-depth investigation composed of interviews, investigating the details of the accident, and analyzing the accident scene to determine the steps to recommend for avoiding any future recurrence. The person performing the investigation should be familiar with the mechanics of the industry in which the accident occurred, but also feel free to call in outside experts if necessary, especially if the accident involved a fire or chemical spills. Documentation, including photos, of the entire investigative process is extremely important.

Documentation in the form of a photograph is invaluable as the information in the photo is hard to dispute when investigating an accident. It records the conditions at that exact moment of which may then be hard to verify later. Caution must be taken to make sure that the flash of a bulb does not cause additional danger such as causing a chemical or gas to ignite due to the spark. If items have been moved to aid a victim or gain access to an area, for example, that should be noted and documented also. In photographing the scene, it is necessary to get photos from all sides and from front to back. For smaller objects, a ruler placed next to the item will show the item's scale in terms of length and width. All photographs should be made in color in order to show differences in the types of liquids, paint colors, and minor details that may not show up in simple black and white photos. Finally, details need to be included with the photos to include the name of the item being photographed, where the item was located in relation to the accident scene, who took the photo, whether the item was moved from its original location, the date and time the photo was taken, and the name of the investigator who took the actual photo.

After an accident, the first detail to administer to is to ensure the medical care of anyone injured in the accident. Second, the area around the accident needs to be secured either by roping it off or placing other barriers nearby to prevent access by anyone other than approved personnel. A sketch should be made of the area showing the placement of people, equipment, and machinery in the vicinity at the time of the accident. The designated person in charge should then take control by addressing other concerns people may have regarding the accident. Photos are good documentation to have, as they will capture the scene at that exact point and, taken properly, are difficult to dispute. Samples need to be taken of any material, part, or fiber that may have caused or contributed to the accident. The area should then be reopened to all employees especially those whose presence is required to perform their regular jobs. Any potential witnesses should then be interviewed and documentation made of their statements regarding the accident. Finally, an analysis is conducted as to the potential causes of the accident with a written report to follow and presentations made to the appropriate managers and owners. Included in this report are recommendations to be made regarding preventing a similar accident in the future.

Although photographs can be taken to add to the investigative folder, a **sketch** gives a more detailed picture of the layout of the area immediately after an accident and identifies how each part is related to each other in terms of distance and vicinity. It is important to use graph paper so the layout of the area of the accident is measured and drawn to scale. This gives the investigators a clear understanding of the layout of the scene for analysis days or weeks after cleanup of the scene is underway. Define the value of each square on the graph paper, i.e. one block equals one foot. Indicate the compass direction and commence drawing the largest objects first, then filling in with the smaller objects and finally, indicate the placement of the witnesses at the time of the accident. A key may be helpful if an identification of the items on the graph cannot be made due to lack of space.

Crucial to the investigation are the actual **samples** taken from the scene, as they may be a determining factor to the cause of an accident. Samples need to be taken as quickly as possible because liquids may evaporate or "run off" the area, or may be inadvertently cleaned up. Also, any vapor or gases may dissipate quickly and their presence may need to be confirmed. When obtaining samples, solids materials need to be placed in a plastic bag, labeled, and sealed. Liquids need to be placed in bottles and also labeled and sealed. The labels should include the information such as the name of the person collecting the sample, the date and time, and the location where the sample was retrieved. Any debris found in the samples need to be submitted along with the sample since cleaning the sample could result in compromising the integrity of the sample and rendering it useless.

All the evidence, interviews, photographs, etc. must be evaluated in order to make a determination as to the cause of an accident. The analysis begins with identifying the direct cause, the indirect cause, the basic cause, and finally any other unsafe acts or conditions which led to the accident. A direct cause is defined as any main contributing factor to causing the accident. Examples of direct causes include being struck against or struck by an object, a fall, an abrasion, contact with a portion of the body, or contact with a toxic substance. After identifying the direct cause, then the indirect cause must be determined. An indirect cause is any unsafe act that is related to the direct cause, which contributes a lesser part to the accident. These can include attempting to perform service or maintenance operations on a machine while it is still in motion, horseplay, failure to wear proper safety equipment, or using equipment in a method for which it is not designed. Finally, basic causes of an accident can include any acts of negligence by someone who was not present during the accident. Examples include lack of proper safety training, inadequate codes or maintenance of the machinery.

Several types of people who were present during the time of the accident will need to be interviewed to make the investigation complete. The people who were witnesses to the accident, the people who were among the first to arrive on the scene of an accident, the people who saw the events that led up to the accident, and the people who have knowledge of the work habits of the person involved in the accident all need to be interviewed. In conducting these interviews, it must be stressed that the investigator is not there to place blame on any individual, but rather to identify the cause of the accident and prevent a similar one from occurring in the future. Witnesses should be interviewed as soon as possible after the accident to prevent loss of detail of what the person saw, as well as prevent any biased information from coming out in the interview as a result of talking to other witnesses. Refrain from asking any leading questions and conduct the interview at a comfortable pace for the witness. Recording the interview is preferred, but if not able to, then detailed note taking after the interview is recommended.

In order to protect the interests of all persons involved in an accident, it is important to ensure that all steps have been followed in properly investigating the accident to avoid any exposure to legal problems. It is important that an accident be investigated as promptly as possible in order to maintain the highest degree of accuracy in collecting evidence. As time passes, evidence may be lost or contaminated during the collection procedure. All evidence must be properly identified with date and time labels. Evidence should also include a description of the item. Photographs, sketches, and other documentation must also be similarly labeled. All witnesses providing statements need to have their statements recorded and approved by the witness prior to adding to the investigative folder. If this is not possible, then a written interview synopsis must be made and signed off by the witness as to its accuracy. An attorney must be consulted prior to testing materials obtained as samples and an independent third party be hired to analyze and provide the results. In the unlikely event that an investigator is unable to perform his or her job due to backlash on behalf of a witness or company, then a court order may be imposed to enable them to do their job.

Once the accident report is completed, it should be submitted to management. The final report should include information answering the basic questions of who, what, when, where, and why. The outline of the report should be in chronological order beginning with where and when the accident occurred, and whom it affected. Also, identification should be made of all witnesses to the accident. Next, a description of the accident in the form of a timeline should be included with a damage report of the injuries as well as the extent of the damage to the facility. Finally, a section covering the direct, indirect and basic causes of the accident should be identified with the last section listing any recommendations on behalf of the investigator to prevent similar accidents.

Safe Lifting Practices

During remediation, it is important to prevent the occurrence of injuries. For lifting heavy objects, the three components that make up safe lifting practices include the pre-lift, lifting, and setting down. When performing the pre-lift, the individual should be aware of the space around him, ensuring that no objects are around which could cause him to lose his footing. Additionally, he should check the item to be lifted for no jagged edges or protruding spots that could cause a person to lose his grip on the object. Performing a partial lift to determine if the balance is correct and also to determine if the object requires more than one person to manipulate. During the actual lift, it is important to have secure footing and lean in close to the object. Keeping the back straight and making slow deliberate movements rather than quick jerks will reduce the occurrence of back injuries. In setting down the object, again, controlled movement is key.

With medical costs on the rise, companies are finding that in order to reduce the occurrence of injuries, safety training is necessary. Back injuries due to improper lifting are on the increase in this country. OSHA has determined that back injuries are the number one problem for workplace safety and over 75 million Americans suffer some degree of back pain preventing them from performing their responsibilities at work. Three components make up safe lifting procedures: pre-lift, lifting, and setting down. As an alternative to lifting, other options exist for transporting heavy loads. One option is to ask another person for assistance with lifting to minimize the stress load each person is carrying. The second option is to transport items using some type of cart on wheels, whether it is a push cart, dolly, two-wheeler, or flatbed.

Confined Spaces Important Terms

Engulfment: A person is subjected to engulfment when any substance such as a liquid, solid, or gas traps an individual inside a confined space and causes them to require rescue assistance in removing the person from the confined space. These substances have the potential to interfere with the person's respiratory function, or the substance can cause the person to become strangled, constricted, or crushed inside the space.

Hazardous Atmosphere: Any atmosphere that has high risk potential to cause incapacitation, loss of consciousness, death, or the inability to rescue oneself from the confines of this space. Less severe risks include injuries or acute illness from exposure to these hazardous chemicals. General causes of these types of hazards include flammable gases or vapors in excess of 10% of its lowest flammable limit (LFL). Airborne combustible dusts that exceeds its LFL or oxygen concentrations that are less than 19.5% or greater than 23.5%.

Confined Space: An area in which the space is large enough for a human being to enter, but is not designed for continuous use. This space does not contain nor have the ability to contain any hazard that can be cause respiratory distress or be deemed fatal to the employee who enters. There are usually limited restrictions into this area.

Permit-Required Confined Space: An area that is again large enough for an employee, however, this space does have the potential for creating a hostile environment in which the health and life of a person could be compromised. The configuration of this space also has the capability of trapping an individual through use of increasingly narrow walls or floor.

Authorized Entrant: A person who has been authorized by their employer to enter this space with an approved permit.

Attendant: An individual who is standing outside of a permit-required confined space to assist the other individual who is inside.

Entry Permit: A document that outlines the purpose for entry into the confined spaces, the individuals who are approved for entry or attending, the type of tests being performed and the schematics of the confined space.

Blanking and blinding: Refers to the process of completely covering the opening of a pipe, line or duct. Using a blank, or blind, this solid piece of material is then installed close to the confined area in order to prevent anything from getting through. It must be strong enough to withstand the maximum pressure forced through the line. The purpose of the installation of this blank must be indicated on a label situated close to the blank for future reference.

Double block and bleed: Involves the use of two valves and one open vent valve to prevent any leakage into a confined space.

Line breaking: The action of completely disconnecting a pipe from use through misalignment or of removing the pipe from the system flow. A disconnected pipe should be tested to insure that no toxic residue or leakage is present.

AIR QUALITY

Using a calibrated direct-reading instrument, an individual can determine the air quality within the confined space. The order of the tests to be conducted is important and they are ranked in order of highest importance: amount of oxygen content, presence of any combustible or flammable gases or vapors, any potential toxic air contaminants such as carbon monoxide or methane, and combustible or explosive dusts such as that from food, metal, or wood products. The acceptable range of oxygen content is 19.5% - 23.5%. Above that percentage causes a fire hazard and below that percentage causes loss of consciousness leading up to death. Any combustible gases or vapors can ignite when it exceeds the LFL, or lower flammable level. Toxic gases can be released with little to no odors and can cause death in a matter of minutes. They are also extremely flammable. Dusts from food and metal products, if ground to the right consistency, will also combust and create respiratory concerns.

Prior to entry in a confined space area, the individual must determine whether or not a permit is required for entry due to the hazardous environment that may be inside. If so, then employees must be notified of the condition. Document the certification showing the date, location, purpose, and name of the person providing the certification to enter the confined area. Isolating the space from other areas is necessary as is frequently flushing and ventilating the area to improve and eliminate some of the hazardous conditions. Ensure that all equipment is properly maintained and tested prior to use. Allow for an attendant to be present outside the permit space assisting the individual entering the confined space. Finally, all personnel who are involved in the remediation of the confined space be informed of their duties and be properly trained.

The typical forms of safety equipment that would be needed to work in a confined space are:

- Safety goggles: Protects against gas, fumes, and dust.
- Personal protective clothing: Protects against toxic or other irritating materials.
- Face shield: Protects against gas, fumes, and dust.
- Head protection: Protects against heavy objects striking against the head.
- Hearing protection: Protects hearing against a possible explosion.
- Hand protection: Gloves to protect against irritants or heat exposure.
- Respirator rated at the appropriate classification
- Air purifier system with its own filtration to remove particulate or gaseous matter (Class 1)

- Air supplied respirator such as a self-contained breathing apparatus, a supplied air respirator, or a combination of the two (Class 2)
- Combination of an air purifier system with an air supply system (Class 3)

Attendant Duties

An attendant's role is to ensure the safety of the entrant who is inside the confined space and perform all the necessary duties as described. Their responsibilities are to know the hazards that may be faced by the entrant inside the space. He must also have the ability to identify any signs or symptoms of exposure to any of the hazardous materials. This person must also be able to perform a non-entry rescue of the entrant if called upon. The attendant sometimes monitors several areas with confined spaces but is not allowed to leave the area unless relieved by another trained attendant. Communication with all entrants the attendant is responsible for is necessary throughout the shift in order to make the person aware of any changes that would cause immediate retreat from the confined space. The attendant is also trained to contact emergency rescue personnel in the event the entrant needs assistance in withdrawing from the confined space.

Retrieval Lines

In situations where the risks outweigh the benefits of using a retrieval line, its use is not recommended. Examples would include the elaborate configuration of the confined space that causes the attendant to not be able to pull strongly enough around turns and other obstructions to be able to remove the entrant in an emergency. If projections inside the enclosed space pose a risk to the person being rescued and potentially being injured from striking these projections, then a retrieval line is not recommended. Finally, if an entrant is using an air supplied respirator that has the potential to become entangled in the retrieval line, then the retrieval line is not used. In these cases, alternate means of rescue must be utilized. If no other means of rescue can be performed, then entry into the confined space is then prohibited.

Retrieval Equipment

The rescue equipment must be built to allow the entrant access into the confined space yet be sturdy enough to successfully remove him from the space in the event of an emergency. Any emergency workers and attendants should be able to perform a rescue without entering the confined space themselves through use of the chest harnesses, full body harnesses, mechanical winches, and wristlets to be used in instances where a chest or full body harness is not feasible. The winch is designed to be self-braking and prevent free falls. A tripod is necessary for stabilization. In order to determine what type of retrieval equipment is to be used, several factors must be considered. The first is the size of the opening of the confined space as well as its internal configuration and location of the opening. The second consideration is whether or not a potential rescue would be performed in either a vertical or horizontal position.

Purging

Prior to initiating the ventilation process, it is important to test the air within the confined space to determine the type of gases and fumes are contained within. Use an alignment chart to calculate the minimal amount of time needed to properly purge the area. This is done by determining the volume of the space, noting it on the chart, identifying the capacity of the blower, and reading the number on the chart that corresponds to the correct amount of time required to purge that area. The number of turns or bends and the capacity of the blower determine the actual timeframe in which to purge the area. After the designated purging time has passed, then testing of the atmospheric conditions inside the system should be conducted again and until the air quality levels are such that it is safe for a person to enter the area.

A worker uses purging and ventilation of the air to clear a confined space prior to entry. Through the use of fans and blowers, the area can be cleared of gases and fumes that can be hazardous or fatal. Ventilation also controls the degree of heat or humidity present in the confined space and also helps prevent fires and potential explosions. Three main types of ventilation procedures are used to clear a space: natural ventilation, mechanical ventilation, and mechanical dilution ventilation. Natural ventilation refers to the opening of all available covers in the duct system that will allow fresh air and wind to clear out the space and exhaust the hazardous gases. Mechanical ventilation is used when natural ventilation is not possible. It involves the diluting and exhausting of the air in the confined space with the use of blowers or fans. Mechanical dilution ventilation is the process in which fresh air is pumped into a confined space until the ratio of hazardous gases to fresh air is within acceptable ranges.

Toxicity Concerns

Some conditions require that entry into the chamber be made for the sole purpose of cleaning the interior. If this is the case, then any cleaning should be done to the best of the ability from the exterior. Testing of the atmospheric conditions is necessary prior to entry by the individual doing the cleaning. The appropriate personal protective equipment should be utilized, including safety goggles, face-mask, protective clothing, and gloves. If, after the initial cleaning (as far as possible into the chamber), further tests show that the air quality levels are unacceptable, then purging, cleaning, and ventilating should be repeated. If the levels are still unacceptable, then the entry should be conducted using appropriate respirators and breathing apparatus. Generally, entries at this point are conducted only in cases of emergency where access is mandatory.

Flammable Area Concerns

Before initiating the procedure, it is important to determine what gases and fumes are present in the chamber through the use of a remote air sampling line. Gases that can commonly neutralize the effect of flammability include nitrogen, carbon dioxide, and argon. Any toxic residue or flammable material found on the walls and floor of the chamber need to be cleaned using either water, or hot steam. Steam, however, has the potential for creating a spark hazard so care should be used. Also, time should be allowed for the chamber to cool down from the steam prior to entry. Steam also can cause static electricity within the chamber, so the steam line should be well grounded. It is important to continually monitor the atmospheric conditions during the entire time that a person is inside of the chamber. In the event that conditions become hazardous, then the person should be evacuated immediately and purging and ventilation begin again.

Continuous General vs. Local Exhaust Ventilation

When there is the presence of toxic gases or fumes and work must be performed, the area must be ventilated to provide a continuous flow of fresh air and removal of toxic air. This type of ventilation procedure should also be performed if the air has the potential to develop a higher concentration of toxicity due to evaporation of chemicals or from desorption from walls. General ventilation also helps by diffusing the amount of toxic chemicals in the air from a confined area to one of greater volume. Respirators should be placed in areas where an emergency exit cannot occur quickly to assist those who need additional time to vacate the area in the event of higher levels of hazardous chemicals. Local exhaust ventilation is used in areas where general ventilation is not feasible. This can be due to working in confined spaces and performing actions such as painting, welding, and cleaning, where the highest concentration of toxic fumes are located in close vicinity to the worker. Use of a respirator is recommended in addition to local ventilation.

Air Quality

The ventilation system must be outfitted with an alarm system to notify the employees of a breakdown and leakage of toxic gases and fumes. Testing of the air quality is important both at the beginning of the project, at the start of each shift and periodically throughout the shift to ensure that the safety of the employees is of top priority. The exhaust of the contaminated air should be made in such a way as to not jeopardize the air quality around the containment area. In areas where the presence of flammable gas, fumes, or substances is present, all electrical equipment must comply with requirements and standards designed to prevent accidents. If ongoing ventilation cannot be performed, then periodic tests must be conducted on the air until regular air quality acceptable levels are maintained.

Lockout/Tagout Procedures

Depending on the type of confinement space that is required, lockout/tagout procedures will be customized for that area according to the project leader. Documentation is required on all points where blanks or blinds have been installed with these records open for inspection. Any air pumps or compressors involved in these areas must be locked out to avoid accidental activation. Shutoff valves will also be tagged and placed in the off position. All electrical systems that service that confined area will need to be turned off and padlocked at the circuit breaker and the corresponding key kept with the individual inside the confined space. Additionally, all mechanical units should be shut down to avoid any injury to the person by removing any drive belts or chains.

Cleaning Tools

Any tools used in cleaning in a confined space must meet the requirements of inspection and maintenance. Commonly used tools include standard hand tools and portable electric tools that have been equipped with a ground fault circuit interrupter. Lighting is also required to be grounded and meet industry standards for use in this area. Lighting used in a confined space should be equipped with a guard and have explosion proof design features. Electric cords used in this confined space must also be inspected prior to use for any defects in the insulation or exposed wiring. Combustible cylinders are prohibited from being used in the confined workspace. Any ladders or scaffolding must be adequately secured in place to prevent toppling over and causing accidents to the workers in the vicinity. Finally, any hose lines that are used must contain a pressure release valve located outside the confinement area.

Cleaning Methods

Any procedures designed to clean the interior of a confined space should be pre-approved by a designated person in charge of the entire remediation process. The specific method to be used is determined by the type of contaminants found in the enclosure. For example, if the air inside the enclosed space were found to contain a high degree of flammable gases, then the cleaning process would reflect the safest method recommended for that particular substance. The area would first be purged of the toxic gas, and then ventilated to bring the air quality back to an acceptable level. Initial cleaning of this confined space would be performed from the outside in as much detail as possible prior to entry. Cleaning methods using steam require specific safety precautions. Steam cleaning produces high temperatures, so a waiting period prior to entry is desired. Additionally, the high temperature levels cause the potential for igniting a spark or flame.

Disciplinary Issues

With the extreme dangerous nature of the business of HVAC remediation, safety is of top concern. It is an ongoing training process designed to protect the health, well being and safety of occupants, employees, contractors, building owners, property, and facilities. Adherence to safety regulations mandated by local, state, and federal regulations must be followed on each job. When situations arise that are violations of safety protocol, proper disciplinary measures must be taken. Common procedures to follow include giving a verbal warning to the employee who committed the safety violation. The second step would be to provide written warnings documented and included in the employee's file. The next steps would be to impose disciplinary suspension and finally, termination of employment. Safety requirements are not to be taken lightly and violations of these regulations could injure or harm another person or property to the extent that fatalities could occur.

Electrical Safety

Important terms:

Circuit: Energy moving from a power source, load, and then back to the beginning forms a continuous loop known as a circuit. A simplistic example involves a battery at one end supplying the power source, leading to a light bulb, which switches on, and then the resulting energy is looped back towards the battery to complete the actual circuit.

Ground: Electric current is connected to other conductive surfaces and the energy is dispersed to help eliminate the accidental spread of too much energy in one area causing an overload of a circuit and also helping to maintain a safer environment.

Switch: A device that allows one to stop or resume the flow of electric current through a wire. This switch automatically shuts off the flow when the circuit is overloaded with current. The end user can restore power through flipping the switch back.

Voltage: The pressure that causes the flow of electric current. The amount of voltage used is proportionately related to the amount of energy required from the object needing power. Common sources of voltage exist in batteries, transformers, and generators.

For trained personnel with experience in working with electric parts, circuits, or electronic equipment, the following guidelines apply in maintaining a sa**fe distance from live current:**

0 – 300 volts = avoid all contact
301v – 700v = maintain a one foot gap
750v – 2kilovolts = one foot, six inches gap
2kv – 15kv = two foot gap
15kv – 37kv = three foot gap
37k – 87kv = three feet, six inches gap
87.5kv – 121kv = four foot gap
121kv – 140kv = four feet, six inches gap

Any untrained employees or personnel in the area of electric equipment are required to maintain a distance of ten feet from all circuits, equipment, and electronic parts.

Electrical Current Effects

With the widespread use of electricity in our homes and businesses, it is important to recognize the dangers that can result from poor training and lack of knowledge in the use and maintenance of electrical equipment. Ensuring that proper grounding occurs when working with "live" wires is important due to the human body being a conductor of electricity. Shock can occur if a live component and a conductive surface are touch at precisely the same time. The effects of shock depend on the amount of current traveling through the wires and can cause the body to twitch slightly or convulse due to a heart attack, possibly leading to death. Minor to severe burns can also occur due to the amount of electrical current traveling through the body. Prior to any work on an electrical component, it is important to shut off all power sent to the system and to discharge any pent up energy stored within.

High Electrical Voltage Areas

In order to safely work in an area of high voltage, the following steps must be taken. First, all sources of power must be identified and located in or near the facility. Second, all personnel must be notified as to the work that will be performed in the area. The machinery or other equipment should be shut down with all equipment disconnected from the power source. All personnel working on a particular piece of equipment must perform the appropriate lockout/tagout procedure and then dissipate any stored up energy. After the work has been completed, then the employee should clear the area of all tools, etc that were used during the work process and clean up any leftover material. Lockout/tagout procedures should be reversed and the machinery or equipment reenergized prior to resuming all operations.

Qualified vs. Unqualified Employees

A person who is considered trained and qualified to work around electrical components is one who is familiar with the hazards associated with electricity and the damage unsafe practices can cause. Training in avoiding those hazards as well as the correct procedures in working with de-energized parts and live electric components is an important aspect of this standard. This person may be trained in certain pieces of machinery and lockout/tagout procedures, but not in others. Thus, in certain scenarios, this person is qualified for work in one area, but not in others where knowledge of the hazards and risks may not be known. As such, this same individual becomes unqualified in that regard. Acceptable training methods can result from both on the job and classroom instruction. The training must include identification of electrical components, live wires, determining voltages, and the distance required for safe clearance.

Safe Environments

According to the Bureau of Labor Statistics, 9% of workplace injuries in 1989 that ended in death were the direct result of electrocution. OSHA recognized the need for a comprehensive set of regulations to outline the procedures to follow when working with electrical components and parts to decrease the risk of injury or death. In 1990, the Electrical Safety Related Work Practices Standard was created to meet this need. In it, it includes the necessary training and precautions for those employees working in areas where the risk of shock, burns, or electrocution is greatest. This standard is for employees who work with voltage levels of 50 or higher where grounding is necessary. Although lockout/tagout procedures are an important part of safety training, they do not ensure complete protection from electrocution. Dispersion of stored energy in mechanical components is a large part of creating a safer work environment.

Safety Measures

Portable electric equipment is defined as those pieces that are transported from one job site to another with the purpose of assisting with any inspection, remediation, maintenance, and repair project. This includes the use of any surge protectors, electrical extension cords, and any plugs. Before initiating work with these components, it is important that a safety checklist be followed. This includes visual inspection to check for frayed or torn cords. Checking for a ground fault circuit interrupter is present as an added measure of protection. Ensuring that there is a proper length of cording, as it is not recommended to hang or lower a piece of equipment by it's cord. When securing the excess cord, it is also not recommended to adhere it by stapling the cord into place. There exists the potential for damaging the electric cover. Finally, it is important that electric cords be approved for use in wet areas if this is where the work is to be performed.

Before a person can set foot in a hazardous area, all mechanical and electric components must be **de-energized** and the stored-up energy released. In the event that machinery is activated while a person is in the vicinity, there is a high risk of injury or death. Any inspections, cleanings, or repair work can only resume when the release of energy has been completed. In addition, lockout/tagout procedures must be followed and if any piece has been de-energized, but the lockout/tagout has not been performed, then it must be assumed that the machinery is still considered "live" and treated with extreme caution. A few instances arise when it is not possible to completely shut down and de-energize the system as in life support systems in hospitals or health care environments, or where the shutting down will cause other adverse effects on the building's occupants. Also, some systems require that maintaining the circuit "live" is necessary for further testing. Safety barricades and warning signs should be posted in the immediate vicinity.

Electrical Hazards

With the extreme hazards of improper handling of electricity, the most common dangers to be encountered include electric shock, burns, arc-blasts, explosions, and fires. Electric shock can be either direct or indirect. Direct shock, by definition, occurs when a person becomes a part of the pathway through which electrons flow. Currents of 30mA or less are capable of causing a fatality. Indirect shock is the end result of when a person receives an electric shock and then as a result of the shock falls from a ladder, scaffold, high ledge, or falls onto a piece of machinery causing injury or death. Burns usually occur on the hands as a result of the person inadvertently touching a "hot" wire or electric component. Finally, arc-blasts occur when an abnormal current flow connects between two points. This arc-blast has the potential to reach up to 35,000v F.

Electrical Explosions and Fires

Although OSHA provides guidelines for the prevention of fire related hazards in working around electricity, the possibility exists for the occurrence of fires and explosions. Through purging and ventilation, the hazardous flammable gases and fumes are exhausted away from the work site; however, the possibility still exists for an explosive situation to occur. Electricity and electrical sparks are the common causes of igniting a fire. Ignition can also occur when electrical components overheat or the warning system fails to notify the workers of hazardous conditions. Fires can also occur when modifications have been made to the wiring, equipment is defective or has been used in an unsafe manner. Stripped wiring or connections to switches and receptacle outlets have also been known to contribute to fires.

Arc-Blast Dangers

With the extreme temperatures encountered in an arc-blast, three primary dangers come into play. Terminal radiation can occur from the arc blast that can cause severe burns depending on the proximity of the worker to the blast. The skin color, type of clothing, amount of personal protective equipment, and amount of exposed skin will help determine the rehabilitation rate of the burn victim. A second danger exists in the pressure wave that presents itself alongside the arc-blast. Pressure waves can be rated at over several hundred pounds of pressure onto a human body depending on the voltage of the arc. The injuries sustained can consist of concussions, broken bones, hearing loss, memory loss, and even death if the person is forced onto a hard object causing blunt force trauma. Finally, a third danger with arc-blasts results from the potential of projectiles to be forced in the direction of the workers. Some examples would be any object in close vicinity that was not strapped down such as power tools, equipment, etc. or even portions of a wall that was blown apart which could become airborne. Additionally, the high temperature of the arc-blast causes steel and aluminum to become molten and the resulting pressure wave forces these droplets outside the blast area, causing severe burns and occasional fires as a result.

Safety Training

All employees immediately upon hire should be trained on the proper safety procedures of their job. This training should also commence when new chemicals are brought into the facility and on an annual basis thereafter. The training to be covered during these sessions should include what is contained within SDS and the types of chemicals covered, the exact location of the hazardous chemicals onsite, and identification of the substance by color, smell, and texture. The training also includes specific hazards associated with this chemical, and any symptoms that can occur due to overexposure. The appropriate medical treatment is included on how to treat a victim of the exposure. Finally, any detection methods used to identify any potential leaks of the substance are also included as is the specific types of protective equipment used when handling this substance.

Fire Prevention

In most facilities, certain areas have an increased risk of fire potential. These can include places where temporary heaters are used, housekeeping closets where high concentrations of flammable cleaning supplies are stored, welding and cutting stations, and trash receptacles, where rags soaked with oil or chemicals may have been tossed. It is important to clean the facility on a daily basis in order to remove chemical residue from floors, surfaces, and machinery. Proper storage of chemicals and flammable liquids must be made in appropriate containers designated for their specific use to avoid any cross contamination. Safety containers can be equipped with a flash arrester to deter the spread of flames. Each workspace must post clear direction to employees on the nearest location of fire extinguishers and emergency exit procedures. Walkways must be clear of any debris and storage that would be a hazard to a quick evacuation. Proper ventilation should be utilized to prevent the build-up of material that can combust in work areas.

Temporary Heating Devices

While trying to ensure the comfort of workers and occupants, use of a temporary heating device must follow certain safety precautions to ensure that the safety of the occupants is not put at adverse risk. Proper ventilation is important and it can be obtained through the use of natural or mechanical means. Appropriate distances must be maintained on all sides from the heating device to ensure that contact of the heating element is not made with any flammable or combustible material. The use of the heater must be maintained at an upright level and the potential for tipping over of the device is reduced. Some types of heaters that utilize solid fuel are prohibited in use in buildings or scaffoldings. A liquid fueled heater should be equipped with an appropriate safety device in the event the flame goes out. All heating devices should be continuously monitored to prevent accidental ignition of flammable materials.

Safety Program Components

In order to effectively manage the safety and well being of the employees, a company has an obligation to create a program that addresses the need for education and prevention of hazardous practices. A designated safety committee needs to be formed with the responsibilities as follows: to educate the employees of the facility, to conduct safety training, provide proper communication regarding best safety practices in both written and oral form, to provide operator training on all machinery, ensure that proper tools are made available and to follow up on inspection and maintenance of critical tools and equipment. Additional responsibilities include personal safety equipment, clothing, headgear, safety glasses, etc. to perform all the necessary jobs on the worksite. The safety committee is responsible for ensuring proper documentation on all onsite accidents. Also, maintenance of the facilities and equipment to prevent causes of accidents falls under their jurisdiction. Finally, the safety committee is to evaluate all existing personal and procedures and provide initial medical care in the event of an accident.

Fire Extinguisher Ratings

The appropriate extinguisher should be in close proximity to the areas where it can be of the most use. The rating system that is printed on the side of a fire extinguisher utilizes color and photos to identify what materials it is able to extinguish. A Class A extinguisher is rated for ordinary combustible materials and the corresponding letter is colored green. Its symbol is a triangle. Class B extinguishers use a red square and are designed for flammable liquids. Class C extinguishers are for putting out electrical fires and the symbol is a blue circle. Class

D extinguishers are designated with a yellow star and are rated for combustible metals. Fire extinguishers can be rated for more than one classification. The appropriate areas that it covers should be labels on the outside of the cylinder with the corresponding symbols listed in a line.

Hazardous Chemical Precautions

When hazardous chemicals enter the facility or worksite, it is important to document their arrival on an inventory sheet to track the chemical and account for its existence. These chemicals must be stored in their original labeled containers to prevent confusion as to their purpose and directions for use. All containers used for hazardous chemicals must be in approved containers designed to prevent leaks and fumes from being released in an improper manner. It is allowed that workers disperse small amounts of the chemical into other containers for use throughout the day; however, any remaining amounts of the chemical must be returned to the original containers at the end of the shift. At no times, should any containers be left unmarked while on premises. Each container, regardless of size, should be labeled in English with the following information: name of the chemical, potential hazard warnings, and the name and address of manufacturer.

A hazardous chemical is any chemical that can cause adverse health effects or can cause a physical hazard such as ignition or explosion. A health hazard is any chemical or substance that is a known carcinogen or toxic substance that when contact is made either through the surface of the skin, inhalation, or ingestion, can cause a person to become violently ill up to and including causing a fatal reaction. Chronic medical conditions may occur due to long term exposure to these chemicals. Specialized personal safety equipment such as protective clothing, gloves, and respirators, can limit the exposure to these risks. A physical hazard is any substance, chemical, gel, gas or vapor that is capable of igniting and contributing to an explosion or fire.

Safety Data Sheets (SDS)

In the event that an appropriate label is not immediately available to identify a potential chemical substance, reference material can be found in a SDS. The information contained within covers:

- Identification of the chemical substance
- Physical and chemical characteristics
- Any health information needed when exposed to this chemical
- Safe exposure limits to this chemical
- Identification of this chemical as a potential carcinogen
- Applicable emergency and first aid procedures
- Name of the group responsible for compiling the SDS information on this chemical

Heat-Related Illnesses

When working in extreme high humidity and temperature conditions, it is important to follow these guidelines to decrease the risk of developing a heat related illness. Expect that under these conditions, work cannot be performed at the same pace as on a more temperate day. Plan on taking nearly double the amount of time to perform the job than usual. Over a period of days, the person's body will become acclimated to the higher temperatures and will be able to perform at a faster rate. All employees and workers are required to stay hydrated throughout the day by drinking a minimum of eight ounces of water per 20-30 minute period. Avoiding all caffeinated, carbonated, and alcoholic beverages helps to keep the body from developing cramps. Using personal protective equipment and clothing with built in temperature controls to aid in cooling the body down will also help avoid heat related illnesses.

Heat stress can occur when working on a job site during conditions where the daily temperature can reach high levels. There are different types of heat related illnesses: heat cramps, heat exhaustion, and heat stroke.

Any physical exertion outdoors in times of high humidity and high temperatures can cause illnesses if not observant of the onset. Heat cramps are muscle spasms that occur when a person sweats profusely and loses a great amount of salt that is not replaced quickly enough. The person may experience severe abdominal pain that may also radiate to other parts of the body such as the arms or legs. Heat exhaustion occurs when a person exhibits extreme sweating and becomes very weak. The person may also vomit or faint, become pale, and the skin become clammy. Heat stroke occurs when a person's body temperature rises very quickly due to the breakdown of their internal temperature regulating system. This person's skin may become red and they may go into convulsions and eventually lose consciousness. Unless prompt treatment is given, there is a high danger of fatalities.

Ladders

Two types of ladders can be found: portable and fixed. Portable ladders can be either adjustable or non-adjustable. Three types of portable ladders include stepladders, single ladders and extension ladders. Guidelines for stepladders are that they be no longer than 20 feet in length. Single ladders are not to be longer than 30 feet, and extension ladders are at maximum length of 60 feet. All ladders should be either lashed or held in place to prevent movement. If a ladder is to be used to gain roof access, then the top point of the ladder should extend at least three feet above the top of the roof structure. Ladders should not be used in the horizontal position to make an improvised scaffold. A worker ascending or descending a ladder should always face the ladder and use each step with the exception of the top step. A person's weight should not be placed on this last step because it can cause the ladder to become unbalanced resulting in a potential fall. Finally, metal ladders should not be in use around electrical equipment or components.

Fixed Ladder Guidelines

A fixed ladder by definition is one that is permanently attached to a building or other structure. A fixed ladder that is a minimum of 20 feet to approximately 30 feet should have a safety barrier in place known as a cage. This cage is designed to protect the worker from a potential fall by enclosing the person who is ascending or descending the ladder. These cages must also extend above the top of the roof structure as an added measure of protection. The ending point of the cage at the bottom of the ladder should be between 7 to 8 feet off the ground. Other types of ladder safety features found in fixed ladders include friction brakes, sliding attachments, and life belts. Oftentimes, fixed ladders come with a landing platform as a designated place of rest during long climbs.

Lockout/Tagout Training

Three categories of employees are required to be trained in lockout/tagout procedures. The first is authorized employees, by which those people whose duty it will be to perform any maintenance or repair work on machinery and who will be the ones to actually provide their names on the back of the tag. The second category is affected employees, meaning those who work in close vicinity of the areas where this work may take place. Although they are not the ones authorized to perform lockout/tagout, they should be made aware of it when they encounter these tags on the worksite. Finally, all other employees should be trained when their work area brings them in close proximity to areas where energy control procedures will be followed. Retraining of lockout/tagout procedures should be made for all these three categories when a person's job has been changed, new equipment has been introduced into the area, or when a change in energy control procedures has been made.

Lockout/tagout is the process by which a person shuts down a piece of machinery or component with the intent to prevent any accidental start-up that could injure a person or cause a fatality. Lockout procedures require that the person who is specifically going to perform maintenance or repair work be the same individual who holds the key to the start-up operations of that piece of machinery. The lock should have a tag attached indicating the name of the person, date, and danger warning signs on it. The tag is designed to inform others that the system is currently inoperable and will not resume until the person performing the work has ended the lockout/tagout procedure. These safety measures are in place so that a person can work on the machine without the fear of another individual inadvertently starting it back up. While performing maintenance or repair work, safety guards may need to be removed and this process ensures that the only person designated to authorize the start-up of a machine is the same person who is authorized to remove the tagout sign.

Lockout/Tagout Procedure

To properly execute the lockout/tagout procedure, the employee should follow these steps:

- Prepare machinery to include identification of all switches, valves, and power sources.
- Know the energy required to shut down the machinery and the process of de-energizing it.
- Notify all affected employees that the lockout/tagout procedure will be performed.
- Perform the standard shut down procedure on that piece of machinery.
- Ensure that all components have their stored energy dissipated.
- Apply the lockout devices to the equipment.
- Retrace the steps to ensure that all controls and switches are in the off - position and are properly locked.
- Check that the equipment is completely disconnected from the power source. Push all equipment and control buttons to ensure their isolation from all power sources and return switches to the off position. The lockout/tagout procedure is now complete.

Work-Related Injuries

Occupational Safety and Health Administration (OSHA) provides for the proper educational and training of employees to ensure a safe work environment. OSHA guidelines do not apply to all businesses. Those with less than 10 employees do not have to provide written documentation on the injuries, illnesses, or accidents on their worksite. For those companies who are not exempt from OSHA recordkeeping, they provide a listing of the required paperwork off their website. The Log of Injury and Illness form, the Injury and Illness Report form, and the Summary Form is required for each year a business is operable. Tracking these accidents can assist with determining the practices that contribute towards an injury, identifying the problem areas in terms of training within a company, and increase awareness of all employees on proper safety practices.

An **injury** is classified as a wound, puncture, stabbing, or other physical damage on the human body through actions encountered while at work. Some examples are falling from a ladder while accessing a rooftop HVAC system, a chemical burn from an arc blast, or dropping a piece of heavy equipment on one's foot at the worksite. Workplace illnesses are identified as those caused by any chemical or irritant that damages the surface of the skin, interferes with respiratory functions, causes problems with hearing or vision, and otherwise poisons the system. Examples of illnesses can include skin disorders such as eczema or rashes from contact with chemicals, respiratory illness such as occupational asthma or bronchitis from breathing contaminants in the air, or even heatstroke or frostbite from working in extreme temperature conditions.

An injury or illness is considered to be **work-related** if it occurs while on company premises or if a pre-existing illness is exacerbated by conditions found on the work-site. For purposes of classification, any location in which an employee is required to be to perform work duties, and an injury occurs, that injury is most likely be classified as work related. Common recordable injuries can include loss of consciousness, fractures, sprains, loss of life, cancer, or any illness made worse through work-related conditions. Additionally, any punctures, scrapes, hearing loss, blood, loss, or damage to one's eyes. This list is not all-inclusive. Also, any injuries requiring medical attention beyond the first aid given at the company work site needs to be recorded on OSHA logs. These logs are specific to each work site and location to help identify trends in accident related injuries at the workplace.

The **incidence rate** is defined as the number of recordable injuries and illnesses that occur at a worksite for a given year within a set number of employees. It is used to compare one company's safety record with those of other businesses within the same industry or to compare data from one year to another. To reach this number, first track all recordable accidents leading to injuries and illnesses on the OSHA log. Then, selecting the number of injuries or illnesses, divide that by the total number of hours worked of all employees, then multiply the total by 200,000 hours equals the total recordable case rate. In order to track other criteria such as the number of fractures, falls, or respiratory illnesses, then you can substitute those numbers in the formula to arrive at the case rate for those incidences.

Personal Protective Equipment Regulations

The intent of utilizing personal protective equipment is not to use it as a substitute for proper safety measures, engineering controls, or other barriers. It is designed to be an additional measure of protection while performing remediation procedures. All clothing, respirators, safety goggles, masks, gloves, etc. are designed to protect the occupant from any potential hazards that may be encountered on the job. These pieces of equipment should be inspected and maintained on a regular basis and disposed of when they are not functioning in the manner in which they are designed. Training on the use of this equipment is required before its use and certification is recommended. A representative of management is responsible for ensuring that employees complete their training prior to use.

Industrial Hygiene Maintenance

Industrial hygiene maintenance refers to a surveillance program where the safety of the employees is monitored on a continuous basis for protection from toxins and hazards. This program monitors those substances that have the potential to cause harm to their employees through overexposure. Also, a time weighted analysis can be performed that can determine safe levels of exposure during regular work activities. It also can determine the correct type of respirator to be used depending on the type of toxin and the degree of contamination levels. This monitoring should be done on all types of job classifications. It can also advise of the proper engineering controls that can reduce or eliminate the level of exposure on the employees. At times, a conservative estimate of the duration of exposure to these contaminations should be made to further protect the employees.

Eye and Face Protection

In order to preserve sight and prevent any physical injuries caused by flying parts, safety goggles and shields are rated for use against different types of contaminants. Goggles can be rated for the amount of force exerted upon them. They also can be outfitted for a person's prescription or worn over regular prescription glasses. Side protection is optional, as some situations do not call for the additional level of protection. Face shields can be full face or partial. Goggles are required under all types of face shields as an additional measure of protection. Welding masks are fitted with a screen at different levels of darkness to allow for work to be performed but also to protect one's vision from the bright glare of the flame. There are different recommendations for filters on the masks depending whether one is welding, using a torch, or using a plasma cutter.

When performing work responsibilities where there is a high degree of particles, matter, and other debris flying through the air, it is important to select eye and face protection appropriate to the type of matter that the employee is working with. Generally, smaller particles that can be inhaled need to be protected against through use of a breathing shield or respirator. Safety glasses should be used if there is a chance of these particles moving about at high velocity. A full-face shield is used if the debris is large enough to cause cuts on the skin from metal parts flying off during a cutting procedure. Other face-shields are designed to protect against hot metal particles that become airborne, or against chemical burns caused by splashing. Goggles are required underneath a face shield as an added measure of protection. The type of work performed, as well as the worksite manager's authorization, is required to determine which safety gear is recommended.

Respirator Use

Before randomly assigning employees to the use of a respirator, the management or safety committee must determine whether there is a valid reason for requiring respirator use in a particular area. The basis for this determination lies in the evaluation of the air quality in an area and determining if the quality is such that respiratory protection is mandated for the safety of the employees. The type of respirator, dust mask, or SCBA will depend on the level and degree of airborne contamination. Respirators should not be assigned to more than one person's use to prevent any cross contamination and when not in use, stored in a clean sanitary location. They should also be clean and disinfected after every use as an added precaution.

Any work activity that involves a person being in close vicinity to airborne particles requires the use of a respirator. With the many types to choose from, the best method for using the appropriate one is to consider the size of the airborne particles one will encounter and also the potential toxicity of the particles themselves. Respirators will be used around construction areas where particles may be released through construction activity, through the transportation of chemicals where fumes and gases may be released from the container, and also in areas near confined spaces where diffusion of a chemical does not occur in sufficient quantities and the contaminants are still airborne. Also, particles may become airborne in the event of a workplace accident or chemical spill. Respiratory protection is used in the even of a fire.

Written Respiratory Protection Programs

When use of respiratory protection is necessary, written procedures should be in place regarding their use and care. These requirements are as follows:

- proper selection of respiratory protection
- a medical evaluation performed on those people who require respiratory protection to perform their jobs
- training on how to ensure a proper fit of all respiratory protection
- cleaning, disinfecting, storing, maintaining, and repair procedures for personal respiratory equipment
- knowledge of when to discard used respiratory equipment that is no longer functioning properly
- procedures for ensuring that SCBA have proper air flow and filtration
- a system in place for evaluating the success of the program

Respirator Contraindications

The following health conditions may contribute in some form to a person being denied ability to use a respirator on the job:

- Diabetes
- Alcoholism
- Asthma
- Pneumonia
- Bronchitis
- Epilepsy
- Skin conditions
- Cardiac disease
- Reduced pulmonary function
- Hypertension
- Anemia
- Claustrophobia
- Use of certain medications
- Hypertension

Medical Evaluations

A physician will determine if a person is physically and psychologically capable of using a respiratory device through an evaluation of all personnel who will require one in order to perform the duties of his position. The individual will first complete a health questionnaire to provide the physician with background health information. Then, the physician will evaluate the person to determine if there are any physiological barriers to the use of the respirator. Some respirators weigh in excess of 35 lbs. when you account for the air tank also. The resulting negative pressure when a person exhales into the respirator takes some time to become acclimated to the distinct breathing process. Finally, the physician will look for any past respiratory conditions such as bronchitis or asthma, which may rule out the potential for successful wear of the respirator. After completing the evaluation, the physician will authorize or reject use of the respirator device for that person.

Respirator Criteria

The selection of a respirator is dependent on several factors. Initially, it is important to identify the type of contaminant within whether it is comprised of gases, vapors, dust, fumes, mold, or other bacteria. Second, the degree of the concentration of the contaminant is important because respirators are made with varying levels of filtration. Another consideration is to determine the acceptable exposure limits of the contaminant. Determining whether or not a substance is an immediate danger to a human life or his/her health is an important consideration of the level of protection a respirator can provide. The flammability of a contaminant is also to be investigated to see if there is a potential for an explosion or fire due to the contaminant coming in contact with dust particles or with another source of ignition. To further protect the worker, it must be determined if the contaminant poses a hazard to the person's vision. If so, then a full-face shield must be considered along with the respirator. Finally, with respirators being manufactured in various sizes, it is possible to obtain a secure fit for each member of the work crew.

Mechanical Filter Respirators

Mechanical filtered respirators come in four different styles: quarter mask, half mask, full face, and disposable. These also come with either a single filter or twin filters. Selecting the proper one depends upon how often the respirator will be used, the type of contamination one can expect to encounter, and also how severe the environmental conditions are. Of primary concern are the MUC (maximum use concentration) and the PEL (permissible exposure limit) of each respirator selected. The MUC is determined according to the types of contaminants present in the environment and the style of the facemask. The standard limitation is ten times the PEL for a disposable, quarter, and half mask, while one hundred times is the limit of a full-face mask. These mechanical filter respirators are not recommended for use in areas where hazards to one's life are immediately present or when there is an oxygen concentration of less than 19.5 %.

Air-Line Respirator

Air-line respirators are comprised of a half mask with a full-face shield, a hood or a helmet, and an air-line hose to convey air to the wearer, and a portable tank that is used as a backup air supply. The air hose supplies air either in a constant flow or only at times when the wearer inhales. At all times, the mask must be kept in constant positive pressure. This type of respirator is designed for use in environments where the percentage of oxygen is below 19.5% or there is a danger to life or health provided that there is a separate tank of auxiliary air serving as a backup in the event the primary system fails. Constant monitoring and presence of an alarm system is required to ensure that buildup of excess carbon dioxide does not occur. The maximum length of hose that is allowed with an air-line respirator is 300 feet. The type of hose must be approved through NIOSH/MSHA.

Chemical Cartridge Respirators

Chemical cartridge respirators generally protect against airborne contaminants comprised of gases, vapors, pesticides, mists, etc. some of which may contain alkaline, acids, mercury, and paint vapors mixed with dust. A half mask is rated for use of ten times the PEL, while the full mask is rated for one hundred times the PEL. Chemical cartridge respirators should not be used in environments where a person's life may be at risk or when the oxygen levels are below 19.5%. Additionally, this specific type of respirator should not be used where air contaminants are odorless and therefore much harder to detect. Each cartridge is labeled to identify the type of contaminant it protects against. Selection of the proper cartridge is important as each only protects against the contaminant listed on the label.

Qualitative Test Measures

The following tests aid in determining whether or not a respirator fits an individual's face properly.

- Negative Pressure Test – Involves physically closing or blocking off all air inlets to the mask and inhaling to determine if there are any leaks. Performed prior to entering a hazardous zone.
- Positive Pressure Test – Also involves the physical closing or blocking off all air inlets, except one exhales, creating a positive pressure in the mask. This test can determine any leaks in the mask.
- Isoamyl Acetate Vapor (banana oil test) – After a respirator device is adjusted to fit, a cloth containing isoamyl acetate is placed closely around the seal of the mask. If the person notices a sweet smell, then there is a leak present around the mask.
- Irritant Smoke Test – A chemical, such as stannic chloride or titanium tetrachloride, is passed in close proximity to the wearer of the face mask causing an involuntary reaction such as coughing or sneezing if there is a leak by which the irritant enters the mask.

SCBAs

A self-contained breathing apparatus (SCBA) is designed to protect the wearer by completely eliminating the need to filter the environment. This system is self-sufficient and relies upon the wearer carrying his own source of oxygen. The system has its own filtration to handle particulate matter as well as processing the carbon dioxide resulting from the wearer's breathing. It can also be used in emergency situations, as it does not allow any air from the hazardous environment to enter the breathing apparatus. This system requires the use of a full-face shield and a separate source of oxygen. Three types of SCBA systems exist: pressure demand open circuit systems, self-generated closed circuit, and compressed oxygen closed circuit apparatus. These types require more extensive training prior to use. The SCBA can provide from 30 minutes to 4 hours worth of breathing time depending on whether the apparatus uses an open or closed circuit.

How to Overcome Test Anxiety

Just the thought of taking a test is enough to make most people a little nervous. A test is an important event that can have a long-term impact on your future, so it's important to take it seriously and it's natural to feel anxious about performing well. But just because anxiety is normal, that doesn't mean that it's helpful in test taking, or that you should simply accept it as part of your life. Anxiety can have a variety of effects. These effects can be mild, like making you feel slightly nervous, or severe, like blocking your ability to focus or remember even a simple detail.

If you experience test anxiety—whether severe or mild—it's important to know how to beat it. To discover this, first you need to understand what causes test anxiety.

Causes of Test Anxiety

While we often think of anxiety as an uncontrollable emotional state, it can actually be caused by simple, practical things. One of the most common causes of test anxiety is that a person does not feel adequately prepared for their test. This feeling can be the result of many different issues such as poor study habits or lack of organization, but the most common culprit is time management. Starting to study too late, failing to organize your study time to cover all of the material, or being distracted while you study will mean that you're not well prepared for the test. This may lead to cramming the night before, which will cause you to be physically and mentally exhausted for the test. Poor time management also contributes to feelings of stress, fear, and hopelessness as you realize you are not well prepared but don't know what to do about it.

Other times, test anxiety is not related to your preparation for the test but comes from unresolved fear. This may be a past failure on a test, or poor performance on tests in general. It may come from comparing yourself to others who seem to be performing better or from the stress of living up to expectations. Anxiety may be driven by fears of the future—how failure on this test would affect your educational and career goals. These fears are often completely irrational, but they can still negatively impact your test performance.

Elements of Test Anxiety

As mentioned earlier, test anxiety is considered to be an emotional state, but it has physical and mental components as well. Sometimes you may not even realize that you are suffering from test anxiety until you notice the physical symptoms. These can include trembling hands, rapid heartbeat, sweating, nausea, and tense muscles. Extreme anxiety may lead to fainting or vomiting. Obviously, any of these symptoms can have a negative impact on testing. It is important to recognize them as soon as they begin to occur so that you can address the problem before it damages your performance.

The mental components of test anxiety include trouble focusing and inability to remember learned information. During a test, your mind is on high alert, which can help you recall information and stay focused for an extended period of time. However, anxiety interferes with your mind's natural processes, causing you to blank out, even on the questions you know well. The strain of testing during anxiety makes it difficult to stay focused, especially on a test that may take several hours. Extreme anxiety can take a huge mental toll, making it difficult not only to recall test information but even to understand the test questions or pull your thoughts together.

Effects of Test Anxiety

Test anxiety is like a disease—if left untreated, it will get progressively worse. Anxiety leads to poor performance, and this reinforces the feelings of fear and failure, which in turn lead to poor performances on subsequent tests. It can grow from a mild nervousness to a crippling condition. If allowed to progress, test anxiety can have a big impact on your schooling, and consequently on your future.

Test anxiety can spread to other parts of your life. Anxiety on tests can become anxiety in any stressful situation, and blanking on a test can turn into panicking in a job situation. But fortunately, you don't have to let anxiety rule your testing and determine your grades. There are a number of relatively simple steps you can take to move past anxiety and function normally on a test and in the rest of life.

Physical Steps for Beating Test Anxiety

While test anxiety is a serious problem, the good news is that it can be overcome. It doesn't have to control your ability to think and remember information. While it may take time, you can begin taking steps today to beat anxiety.

Just as your first hint that you may be struggling with anxiety comes from the physical symptoms, the first step to treating it is also physical. Rest is crucial for having a clear, strong mind. If you are tired, it is much easier to give in to anxiety. But if you establish good sleep habits, your body and mind will be ready to perform optimally, without the strain of exhaustion. Additionally, sleeping well helps you to retain information better, so you're more likely to recall the answers when you see the test questions.

Getting good sleep means more than going to bed on time. It's important to allow your brain time to relax. Take study breaks from time to time so it doesn't get overworked, and don't study right before bed. Take time to rest your mind before trying to rest your body, or you may find it difficult to fall asleep.

Along with sleep, other aspects of physical health are important in preparing for a test. Good nutrition is vital for good brain function. Sugary foods and drinks may give a burst of energy but this burst is followed by a crash, both physically and emotionally. Instead, fuel your body with protein and vitamin-rich foods.

Also, drink plenty of water. Dehydration can lead to headaches and exhaustion, especially if your brain is already under stress from the rigors of the test. Particularly if your test is a long one, drink water during the breaks. And if possible, take an energy-boosting snack to eat between sections.

Along with sleep and diet, a third important part of physical health is exercise. Maintaining a steady workout schedule is helpful, but even taking 5-minute study breaks to walk can help get your blood pumping faster and clear your head. Exercise also releases endorphins, which contribute to a positive feeling and can help combat test anxiety.

When you nurture your physical health, you are also contributing to your mental health. If your body is healthy, your mind is much more likely to be healthy as well. So take time to rest, nourish your body with healthy food and water, and get moving as much as possible. Taking these physical steps will make you stronger and more able to take the mental steps necessary to overcome test anxiety.

Mental Steps for Beating Test Anxiety

Working on the mental side of test anxiety can be more challenging, but as with the physical side, there are clear steps you can take to overcome it. As mentioned earlier, test anxiety often stems from lack of preparation, so the obvious solution is to prepare for the test. Effective studying may be the most important weapon you have for beating test anxiety, but you can and should employ several other mental tools to combat fear.

First, boost your confidence by reminding yourself of past success—tests or projects that you aced. If you're putting as much effort into preparing for this test as you did for those, there's no reason you should expect to fail here. Work hard to prepare; then trust your preparation.

Second, surround yourself with encouraging people. It can be helpful to find a study group, but be sure that the people you're around will encourage a positive attitude. If you spend time with others who are anxious or cynical, this will only contribute to your own anxiety. Look for others who are motivated to study hard from a desire to succeed, not from a fear of failure.

Third, reward yourself. A test is physically and mentally tiring, even without anxiety, and it can be helpful to have something to look forward to. Plan an activity following the test, regardless of the outcome, such as going to a movie or getting ice cream.

When you are taking the test, if you find yourself beginning to feel anxious, remind yourself that you know the material. Visualize successfully completing the test. Then take a few deep, relaxing breaths and return to it. Work through the questions carefully but with confidence, knowing that you are capable of succeeding.

Developing a healthy mental approach to test taking will also aid in other areas of life. Test anxiety affects more than just the actual test—it can be damaging to your mental health and even contribute to depression. It's important to beat test anxiety before it becomes a problem for more than testing.

Study Strategy

Being prepared for the test is necessary to combat anxiety, but what does being prepared look like? You may study for hours on end and still not feel prepared. What you need is a strategy for test prep. The next few pages outline our recommended steps to help you plan out and conquer the challenge of preparation.

Step 1: Scope Out the Test

Learn everything you can about the format (multiple choice, essay, etc.) and what will be on the test. Gather any study materials, course outlines, or sample exams that may be available. Not only will this help you to prepare, but knowing what to expect can help to alleviate test anxiety.

Step 2: Map Out the Material

Look through the textbook or study guide and make note of how many chapters or sections it has. Then divide these over the time you have. For example, if a book has 15 chapters and you have five days to study, you need to cover three chapters each day. Even better, if you have the time, leave an extra day at the end for overall review after you have gone through the material in depth.

If time is limited, you may need to prioritize the material. Look through it and make note of which sections you think you already have a good grasp on, and which need review. While you are studying, skim quickly through the familiar sections and take more time on the challenging parts. Write out your plan so you don't get lost as you go. Having a written plan also helps you feel more in control of the study, so anxiety is less likely to arise from feeling overwhelmed at the amount to cover.

Step 3: Gather Your Tools

Decide what study method works best for you. Do you prefer to highlight in the book as you study and then go back over the highlighted portions? Or do you type out notes of the important information? Or is it helpful to make flashcards that you can carry with you? Assemble the pens, index cards, highlighters, post-it notes, and any other materials you may need so you won't be distracted by getting up to find things while you study.

If you're having a hard time retaining the information or organizing your notes, experiment with different methods. For example, try color-coding by subject with colored pens, highlighters, or post-it notes. If you learn better by hearing, try recording yourself reading your notes so you can listen while in the car, working out, or simply sitting at your desk. Ask a friend to quiz you from your flashcards, or try teaching someone the material to solidify it in your mind.

Step 4: Create Your Environment

It's important to avoid distractions while you study. This includes both the obvious distractions like visitors and the subtle distractions like an uncomfortable chair (or a too-comfortable couch that makes you want to fall asleep). Set up the best study environment possible: good lighting and a comfortable work area. If background music helps you focus, you may want to turn it on, but otherwise keep the room quiet. If you are using a computer to take notes, be sure you don't have any other windows open, especially applications like social media, games, or anything else that could distract you. Silence your phone and turn off notifications. Be sure to keep water close by so you stay hydrated while you study (but avoid unhealthy drinks and snacks).

Also, take into account the best time of day to study. Are you freshest first thing in the morning? Try to set aside some time then to work through the material. Is your mind clearer in the afternoon or evening? Schedule your study session then. Another method is to study at the same time of day that you will take the test, so that your brain gets used to working on the material at that time and will be ready to focus at test time.

Step 5: Study!

Once you have done all the study preparation, it's time to settle into the actual studying. Sit down, take a few moments to settle your mind so you can focus, and begin to follow your study plan. Don't give in to distractions or let yourself procrastinate. This is your time to prepare so you'll be ready to fearlessly approach the test. Make the most of the time and stay focused.

Of course, you don't want to burn out. If you study too long you may find that you're not retaining the information very well. Take regular study breaks. For example, taking five minutes out of every hour to walk briskly, breathing deeply and swinging your arms, can help your mind stay fresh.

As you get to the end of each chapter or section, it's a good idea to do a quick review. Remind yourself of what you learned and work on any difficult parts. When you feel that you've mastered the material, move on to the next part. At the end of your study session, briefly skim through your notes again.

But while review is helpful, cramming last minute is NOT. If at all possible, work ahead so that you won't need to fit all your study into the last day. Cramming overloads your brain with more information than it can process and retain, and your tired mind may struggle to recall even previously learned information when it is overwhelmed with last-minute study. Also, the urgent nature of cramming and the stress placed on your brain contribute to anxiety. You'll be more likely to go to the test feeling unprepared and having trouble thinking clearly.

So don't cram, and don't stay up late before the test, even just to review your notes at a leisurely pace. Your brain needs rest more than it needs to go over the information again. In fact, plan to finish your studies by noon or early afternoon the day before the test. Give your brain the rest of the day to relax or focus on other things, and get a good night's sleep. Then you will be fresh for the test and better able to recall what you've studied.

Step 6: Take a Practice Test

Many courses offer sample tests, either online or in the study materials. This is an excellent resource to check whether you have mastered the material, as well as to prepare for the test format and environment.

Check the test format ahead of time: the number of questions, the type (multiple choice, free response, etc.), and the time limit. Then create a plan for working through them. For example, if you have 30 minutes to take a 60-question test, your limit is 30 seconds per question. Spend less time on the questions you know well so that you can take more time on the difficult ones.

If you have time to take several practice tests, take the first one open book, with no time limit. Work through the questions at your own pace and make sure you fully understand them. Gradually work up to taking a test under test conditions: sit at a desk with all study materials put away and set a timer. Pace yourself to make sure you finish the test with time to spare and go back to check your answers if you have time.

After each test, check your answers. On the questions you missed, be sure you understand why you missed them. Did you misread the question (tests can use tricky wording)? Did you forget the information? Or was it something you hadn't learned? Go back and study any shaky areas that the practice tests reveal.

Taking these tests not only helps with your grade, but also aids in combating test anxiety. If you're already used to the test conditions, you're less likely to worry about it, and working through tests until you're scoring well gives you a confidence boost. Go through the practice tests until you feel comfortable, and then you can go into the test knowing that you're ready for it.

Test Tips

On test day, you should be confident, knowing that you've prepared well and are ready to answer the questions. But aside from preparation, there are several test day strategies you can employ to maximize your performance.

First, as stated before, get a good night's sleep the night before the test (and for several nights before that, if possible). Go into the test with a fresh, alert mind rather than staying up late to study.

Try not to change too much about your normal routine on the day of the test. It's important to eat a nutritious breakfast, but if you normally don't eat breakfast at all, consider eating just a protein bar. If you're a coffee drinker, go ahead and have your normal coffee. Just make sure you time it so that the caffeine doesn't wear off right in the middle of your test. Avoid sugary beverages, and drink enough water to stay hydrated but not so much that you need a restroom break 10 minutes into the test. If your test isn't first thing in the morning, consider going for a walk or doing a light workout before the test to get your blood flowing.

Allow yourself enough time to get ready, and leave for the test with plenty of time to spare so you won't have the anxiety of scrambling to arrive in time. Another reason to be early is to select a good seat. It's helpful to sit away from doors and windows, which can be distracting. Find a good seat, get out your supplies, and settle your mind before the test begins.

When the test begins, start by going over the instructions carefully, even if you already know what to expect. Make sure you avoid any careless mistakes by following the directions.

Then begin working through the questions, pacing yourself as you've practiced. If you're not sure on an answer, don't spend too much time on it, and don't let it shake your confidence. Either skip it and come back later, or eliminate as many wrong answers as possible and guess among the remaining ones. Don't dwell on these questions as you continue—put them out of your mind and focus on what lies ahead.

Be sure to read all of the answer choices, even if you're sure the first one is the right answer. Sometimes you'll find a better one if you keep reading. But don't second-guess yourself if you do immediately know the answer. Your gut instinct is usually right. Don't let test anxiety rob you of the information you know.

If you have time at the end of the test (and if the test format allows), go back and review your answers. Be cautious about changing any, since your first instinct tends to be correct, but make sure you didn't misread any of the questions or accidentally mark the wrong answer choice. Look over any you skipped and make an educated guess.

At the end, leave the test feeling confident. You've done your best, so don't waste time worrying about your performance or wishing you could change anything. Instead, celebrate the successful completion of this test. And finally, use this test to learn how to deal with anxiety even better next time.

Review Video: Test Anxiety
Visit mometrix.com/academy and enter code: 100340

Important Qualification

Not all anxiety is created equal. If your test anxiety is causing major issues in your life beyond the classroom or testing center, or if you are experiencing troubling physical symptoms related to your anxiety, it may be a sign of a serious physiological or psychological condition. If this sounds like your situation, we strongly encourage you to seek professional help.

Online Resources

Due to our efforts to try to keep this book to a manageable length, we've created a link that will give you access to all of your online resources:

mometrix.com/resources719/ascs

It's Your Moment, Let's Celebrate It!

Share your story @mometrixtestpreparation